Hebrews
Personal Workbook

By Chad Sychtysz

Published by
Spiritbuilding Publishers
9700 Ferry Road, Waynesville, Ohio 45068

HEBREWS PERSONAL WORKBOOK
By Chad Sychtysz

ISBN: 978–1–964–80538–2

Spiritbuilding
PUBLISHERS

spiritbuilding.com

Table of Contents

The author of this workbook can be contacted at chad@booksbychad.com

Cover design by Larissa Lynch

Introduction to *Hebrews*

*H*ebrews is one of the most important epistles of the New Testament (NT), taking us deep into the heart of Christ's role as both King and High Priest. The entire epistle radiates with glowing respect for Jesus' lordship and intercession. It gives us rare glimpses into Christ's role as an obedient Son as well as His incalculable offering as the Redeemer of sinful men.

Yet while the writer of *Hebrews* teaches us to adore the Savior, he also forces us to examine our own heart and where we stand with the Lord. Just as he warned his fellow Christians against succumbing to unbelief, so we today must struggle against this same temptation. Those who do not appreciate what Christ has done (and continues to do), or are ignorant of the dangers of unbelief, put themselves in danger of falling away from the truth.

Authority and Authorship: The *Hebrews* epistle has rarely been held as anything but authentic, sacred, and divinely inspired. It has always been considered a part of the apostolic-approved body of writings (a.k.a. the canon) that defines Christian theology and practices. Its doctrines never contradict any of those expressed elsewhere in the NT. The epistle's style—including its reverence, intelligence, authoritativeness, majesty, etc.—is comparable to other established sacred writings, and often exceeds them. When coupled with the other facts concerning this book, such characteristics provide substantial internal evidence for its credibility. It is also found in nearly all (and in the oldest) versions and manuscripts of the NT.

In the earliest compilations of the NT, men grouped *Hebrews* together with the apostle Paul's epistles, indicating that he was its author, but this is difficult to prove. Even the early "fathers" (2nd and 3rd century commentators) disagreed amongst themselves on this. Some believe Paul is the author of *Hebrews* because of the epistle's rabbinic scholarliness. In some Bible translation's, the superscription to the letter reads, "Paul's Epistle to the Hebrews," yet these words are supplied by translators themselves and are not found in the actual manuscripts. Commonly suggested alternative authors include Luke, Barnabas, Apollos, or someone of such caliber as these men.

Whoever did write *Hebrews* reveals a mastery of Old Testament (OT) themes and concepts, as well as NT Christology (i.e., the doctrines of the nature and work of Christ). While we cannot rule out Paul for certain, we cannot prove him to be the author, either. The best approach to the question of authorship is to focus on what we *do* know about him.

❑ He was most likely a Jew himself, being so conversant and capable in discussing Jewish law, covenant, and prophecy.

❑ He has written in "the most perfect Greek,"[1] having a masterful command of the language and its nuances.

❑ He possesses a strong command of the Levitical ministry (i.e., the priestly and sacrificial system of the Law of Moses), the ministry of Christ's own redemptive sacrifice, and an intelligent comparison of the two. He is no novice disciple; he speaks with authority, clarity, and purpose; he is a master communicator.

❑ He speaks of (or with a view toward) the termination of the old (Mosaic or Levitical) system. The primary thesis of this epistle is the superiority of Christ—His sacrifice and its implications—to the Law of Moses and its priesthood.

❑ He does not speak as the founder of the congregation(s) to whom he writes, but as a minister in the field, so to speak. He implies that their original leaders (elders and/or teachers) have since died (13:7), since their present ones are distinguished from them.[2] This indicates a well-established group of older first-generation believers mixed with second- and third-generation believers. The epistles that we know were authored by Paul were written primarily for first-generation believers.

❑ He is a friend of Timothy (13:23), and a teacher well-known to those to whom he writes (13:19). However, he speaks of circumstances which are not described in any of Paul's personal letters to Timothy himself.

If *Hebrews* was written by Paul, then it would have to be written before AD 64, the generally accepted year of his death. The imminent destruction of the Jewish system, the epistle being directed to an older generation of believers, and the struggles that the writer addresses which are common to such people do seem to favor an AD 60s time of writing. However, despite piecing together all the evidence available to us, we still cannot know for certain its date of composition, except that it likely preceded the Jewish revolts against Rome (AD 66 – 70).

Just because *Hebrews* may not have been written by Paul (or another apostle) does not mean that it is not apostolic in nature, sanctioned with apostolic authority, or uninspired by the Holy Spirit. The doctrinal content of the epistle nowhere contradicts what the apostles have written; in fact, it concurs beautifully with (particularly) Paul's and Peter's writings. It is also consistent with what is taught in the Law of Moses: everything the writer explains concerning the Law or its functions (i.e., priesthood, tabernacle, offerings, etc.) can be learned through OT Scripture. Furthermore, the fact that early Christians quoted heavily from *Hebrews* alongside their quotes from Paul and other inspired writers indicates that they believed all such writings carried equal authority.

Who Were the Hebrews? The fact that this epistle was written to Hebrews (Jewish Christians) is obvious. Its recipients were not newcomers to the faith; the epistle is not designed to teach one how to become a Christian. These people had been faithfully teaching, practicing, and supporting the gospel for some time, but had become very discouraged over what they perceived was a lethal assault against the church. In other words, they perceived an overthrow of the church by means of external persecution, and thus were seriously considering abandoning their allegiance to Christ altogether, likely to return fully to Judaism. The several statements implying this, and the fact that the author freely appeals to Hebrew Scripture, implies that the older recipients of this letter were once immersed in the Jewish system. At the time of writing, that system is still in their blood, so to speak. Thus, the overall objective of *Hebrews* is to remind them of their commitment to

Christ, especially since everything He offers is superior to anything they had left behind.

The next logical question, then, would be: *which* Jewish Christians—in what city or area? These people had endured persecution (10:32–34), but it is not clear who it was that persecuted them, whether Jews or Romans. The writer mentions how some had endured "the seizure of your property" (10:34), which is something expected of Roman persecution, not Jewish. If true, this would lean us toward a date of writing after Emperor Nero's persecution of the church in AD 64, when the burning of Rome was blamed upon Christians.[3] There are other subtle hints in the text that point toward a state-sanctioned persecution rather than a religious one (by the Jews).

Theme and Purpose: A dominant theme of *Hebrews* is the supremacy of Christ over the Levitical system (i.e., the priesthood and sacrificial system defined by the Law of Moses). For example, we read of:

- ❑ **the supremacy of Christ in God's plan of redemption for man.** This is mentioned elsewhere (Eph. 1:9–10, 19–23, Col. 1:15–18, etc.), but nowhere is the idea as powerfully and eloquently developed as it is in *Hebrews*.
- ❑ **the supremacy of Christ to Moses.** This epistle shows Christ to be *infinitely superior* to Moses the man <u>and</u> the Law of Moses. This is not a new challenge (John 5:39–47, Acts 3:22–23, etc.), but one which is argued powerfully and thoroughly.
- ❑ **the supremacy of Christ to the Levitical priesthood.** Instead of inheriting a priesthood handed down from and corrupted by men, Christ became a new High Priest of an new order—one not based on a law given to men, but upon God's divine oath.
- ❑ **the supremacy of Christ's blood (life) to that of the ancient sacrifices under the Law.** Animal blood served a purpose in educating Israel in atonement for sin through sacrifice. Yet this kind of blood could not fulfill what God required for the cleansing of a human soul. Christ's blood does fulfill this, however, and provides a complete and final answer to the problem of human sin.

- ❑ **the supremacy of God's covenant with Christians.** God purposely and inherently limited what His covenant with Israel could do. It pointed forward to a "better covenant," one made effective through the blood of Christ. Those who are *now* in a covenant relationship with God ("in Christ") can approach Him with unprecedented access and fellowship.
- ❑ **Christ's supreme obedience to God.** Because of Christ's perfect obedience, He was worthy to inaugurate a new covenant, a new priesthood, and a "new and living way" by which we can come to God (10:20).
- ❑ **Christ's supreme intercession for the believer.** Since He has been made like us—in human form yet without human corruption—Christ serves as the ideal intercessor between God and man (1 Tim. 2:5–6).

Beyond these details of Christ and His redemptive work, *Hebrews* expounds upon other significant perspectives closely associated with these thoughts. It teaches, for example, to:

- ❑ **learn** from the mistakes of an entire generation of Israelites who forfeited their opportunity to enter the Promised Land.
- ❑ **continue** to grow in maturity, not stagnating in useless "elementary" discussions; not subsisting only on "milk" but seeking "solid food" (5:12–13, 6:1–3).
- ❑ **remember** what Christ has done for us; those who have taught us the word of God (13:7); traveling missionaries (13:2); those imprisoned for their faith (13:3); those who have exemplified the kind of faith approved by God (chapter 11); etc.
- ❑ **avoid unbelief** in all its forms but particularly in *doubting Christ's pre-eminence as the Savior of all men.* Failing to believe in the Lord and His gospel will not lead to a believer's "Sabbath rest" (4:9) but God's "terrifying" judgment of him (10:31).
- ❑ **find encouragement** from the "great cloud of witnesses" (12:1), the rich legacy of faithful men and women who provide numerous examples of what it means to live by faith, even during times of great discouragement and opposition.

- **revere God** with all solemnity: "worship God with reverence and awe" (12:28).

In sum, *Hebrews* serves as a series of admonitions to Christians. The author was obviously aware of the danger of deserting the Christian faith and the lack of appreciation that some had for Christ's sacrifice. But he does not merely offer warnings against backsliding; he also explains the *sources* of such decline. These include:

- lack of comprehension of the big-picture perspective.
- tendency to revert to that which is familiar but not better.
- spiritual ignorance due to a lack of careful study of Scripture (5:13 – 6:1).
- spiritual weakness (ineffectiveness) due to spiritual ignorance (12:12–13).
- forgetfulness of earlier exercises of their own great faith (10:32–36).
- forgetfulness of the "faithful" who had preceded them.
- failure to appreciate the new and "unshaken kingdom" (12:27–28).
- failure to see all the benefits and blessings which they had in Christ.

Finally, the writer reminded his readers that "Jesus Christ is the same yesterday and today and forever" (13:8). This statement underlies the entire epistle: since Jesus does not change, then whatever was happening to the Hebrews did not indicate a change in His gospel or a disintegration of His power or authority. It is the Hebrew Christians *themselves* who were changing, not the Lord; *they* were the ones leaving God, even though God promised never to leave them (13:5b–6).

Questions

1.) One huge problem facing the church today is many Christians' failure to *stay committed*. This is true even in places (like America) where there is great prosperity and little persecution. How can *Hebrews* provide a great response to those who struggle with staying focused on Christ?

2.) Please review the above causes of spiritual decline. Are these factors still relevant or have divisive church "issues" and social ills replaced them?

SECTION ONE:
THE SUPREMACY OF CHRIST
(1:1—3:6)

Prelude:
Christ Is Heir of All Things
(1:1–3)

The first verses (1:1–3) acknowledge the majesty and deity of Jesus Christ, who is the subject—directly or indirectly—of this entire work. The opening line (1:1) also assumes the existence and sovereign authority of God: "He is a God who speaks; and, because only a person can speak, this reveals him as a personal God."[4] Every fact we know about God has come to us through His divine revelation. The manner of that revelation, however, has progressed as humankind matured in its understanding.[5] Thus, throughout this epistle, the writer regularly draws significant contrasts to what *was* (i.e., the Law of Moses) and what *now is* (i.e., the gospel of Christ). His opening remarks already illustrate this:

Then	Now
"long ago"	"in these last days"
"in many portions and many ways"	in this one way [implied; see John 14:6]
"[God] spoke to the fathers"	"[God speaks] to us"
"in the prophets"	"in His Son"

The "last days" refer to the Christian era. The context for "last days" has to do with the manner of God's revelation to men (1 Peter 1:20–21).[6] Before Christ ("long ago"), God communicated to men in various ways: prophecies, high priests,[7] dreams, "types," and signs performed among Israel. Now, all essential revelation from God to man has come to us through His Son, Jesus Christ—either directly (by His own words) or indirectly (by His own apostles—see 2 Peter 3:1–2). Before, God's revelation spanned centuries through a slow unfolding and gradual disclosure. Now, in less than a century, God has revealed more than He ever did through the prophets. Jesus Himself is God's supreme revelation to man: the word of God in the flesh (John 1:1–2, 14).

God appointed Christ "heir of all things"—not simply "an" heir but the *sole* Heir (1:2)—since He is God's only begotten Son (John 3:16). All that belongs to God now belongs to Christ.[8] Christ did not take His Father's authority illegitimately, but the Father *gave* all things to Him (Mat. 28:18). He built His church with His Father's full consent and blessing. He could not have begun His church, however, until He "sat down at the right hand" of God in heaven (1:3).

But Christ was not powerless and without authority prior to His ascension to His Father's throne. While we know little of Christ's pre-incarnate existence, we *do* know that all Creation came into existence through Him (John 1:3, Col. 1:15–17). He did this with the power and authority He has always possessed as God (a divine Being). In other words, before Christ was revealed to *us* as God's "Son," He has always existed in *heaven* as one of the Godhead.[9]

Thus, Christ's kingship was not the beginning of His power but marks a particular phase and fulfills a specific need of God's kingdom: as the Redeemer of human souls. The work of God the Son was necessary to accomplish this: His sacrifice, His blood, and His intercession.[10] There is not now and never will be *anyone* comparable to Jesus Christ. He is the Creator of our world, and He is the end (or completion) of God's revelation to man (Rev. 22:13).

Christ is not merely a reflection of God's glory: He is filled with it (1:3a; see John 1:14, Col. 1:19, and 2:9). "Exact representation" means an imprint, stamp, or essential character (of something).[11] Thus, Christ bears the *full, expressed nature* of the Father, reproducing His glory without blurring, distortion, or misinterpretation. While on earth,

Christ provided an accurate portrayal of His Father who dwells in heaven (John 1:18, 10:30). If we have "seen" Christ (in faith), then we have "seen" the Father (John 14:7–10).

Having described who Christ is, the writer now turns to what He has accomplished (1:3b). The "purification of sins" refers to the atoning sacrifice He carried out on the cross. This purification was not for His sins, since He was sinless, but for ours since we cannot approach God otherwise. This describes a priestly action: our having been sprinkled with His blood (1 Peter 1:2) alludes to what was performed by the ancient Levitical priests who made atonement for sins of the sons of Israel (Lev. 1:5, 3:2, 5:6, 16:14, etc.).[12] In this indirect manner, Christ is introduced to us as our High Priest: His is *like* the Levitical priesthood but exceeds it in every respect.

In the OT, the priest's work was always performed standing up, never sitting down. Priests work standing up (offering sacrifices), kings work sitting down (to rule on a throne). Having accomplished all things that God required of a divine High Priest, Christ then took His rightful place next to the Father to rule over His Father's kingdom (1:3b). This necessarily implies the entire *completion* of Christ's ministry since He would never have "sat down" if more redemptive work remained. While the "sitting" here is figurative, it symbolizes two things: the supreme authority of Christ *and* the completion of His redemptive work here upon earth. To summarize:

- ❑ We are in the "last days" of God's revelation to man. There are no more "days" in which new or surpassing revelations will be given.
- ❑ In these "last days," God has spoken to us in His own Son: He is our final authority.
- ❑ God's Son is the exact image of His Father: if we know Christ, we know the Father.
- ❑ He (the Son) is the Creator of all that has begun to exist.
- ❑ He continues to uphold all things by the word of His sovereign power.

- He has made purification (on the cross) for human souls (as our High Priest).
- Having done this, He has sat down at the right hand of the Father (as our King).

Lesson One:
Christ's Supremacy over Angels
(1:3b—2:4)

A More Excellent Name than Angels (1:4–14): Perhaps the writer felt compelled to address angels' inferiority to Christ in response to angelology, the study and worship of angels that was popular among the Jewish elite in the first century (also implied in Col. 2:18). He is "better" not only in worthiness but also in rank; He has "a more excellent name than" any angel; therefore, He deserves more reverence and recognition than them. Christ's "name" indicates His authority, status (as God's Son), and all the attending privileges associated with His position (Phil. 2:9–11). (The quotes in 1:5 are from Psalm 2:7 and 2 Sam. 7:14, respectively.)

God never refers to any angel as His "Son" or His "Begotten"; there is no hint in Scripture of a father-son relationship between God and His angels.[13] However, Christ's sonship to the Father serves as one of the fundamental underpinnings of the gospel (Mat. 16:16).

The writer quotes heavily from the OT to underscore His point.[14] No angel ever held the rank or position of pre-eminence as Christ but instead gives honor and glory to Him. No angel was ever said to occupy a "throne," given a "scepter," or "anointed" by God (1:8–9). These are all kingly terms that have been applied to men (such as David) but are ideally applied to Christ the King, in fulfillment of several prophecies (2 Sam. 7:13–16, Psalm 89:20–21, and Isa. 9:6–7). Also, no angel was ever credited with laying the foundations of the earth or with the creation of the heavens (1;10), but the Son has been credited with all of these (John 1:3, Col. 1:16–17).

"Sitting" does not suggest idleness but (in 1:13) just the opposite: the activity of kingly rule and authority. Christ cites this same OT passage (Psalm 110:1) with reference to Himself (Mat. 22:41–45). For a king to put his feet upon his enemies signifies complete and unconditional superiority over them (see Josh. 10:22–25). But no angel was ever promised such kingship or pre-eminence; we have no record in Scripture of angels sitting (in authority) on thrones. Angels are *authorized* by God to do or say certain things but are never given their own authority as Christ possesses. Angels serve the King (Christ) and His servants on earth (1:14) but are never *compared* to the King and never *minister in place of* Christians.[15] Finally, Christ is never referred to as an angel in Scripture.

The Superiority of What Christ Said (2:1–4): Having established Christ's supremacy to angels, the writer now shows the necessary implications of this (2:1). Since Christ is greater than heavenly angels, what He has revealed (His gospel) is greater than whatever revelation came through angels (the Law of Moses). And if no *angel* can share honor with Christ, then certainly no *man*—not even Moses—can be honored alongside Him, either. This superior message deserves "much closer attention" than what was given to Israel. To "drift away" from it is the result of carelessness and inattention.

The "word" (in 2:2) refers specifically to God's covenant with Israel, which was "spoken" or commanded through angels (see Acts 7:53 and Gal. 3:19). While there is no literal reference to angels speaking the Law to Moses, this has been the mode of God's presentation of Himself to people prior to that.[16] The contrast between how the Law was presented and how Christ's gospel was presented is in how both laws were communicated: one, by angelic intercession; the other, "in His Son" (recall 1:2). Angels were never the source of authority for divine commandments; Christ, however, *is* the source of authority for His teaching (Mat. 7:29, 28:19).

The Law of Moses was binding upon Israel, and disobedience to it warranted serious consequences, including execution. If a law ordained by angels is authoritative and binding, then we will not "escape" divine condemnation for disregarding a "so great a salvation" as ordained by Christ Himself—One who is higher than *all* angels (2:3a). Christ's gospel was confirmed by "those who heard" Him. Most notably, this would be His apostles (2:3b) but may include other preachers as well (Luke 1:1–2).

Finally, this new covenant message—superior to the one ordained by angels in every respect—was confirmed by far more, far different, and far greater miracles than even what Israel had seen at the inauguration of their own covenant. Christ performed "signs and wonders and…various miracles" (as did His apostles—compare John 5:36, 10:37–38, Acts 1:3, and 2 Cor. 12:12), culminating in His resurrection from the dead. Such signs could not be ignored or explained away; even Christ's detractors could not deny them (John 11:47, Acts 4:16, etc.).

As an extension of the signs performed by Christ and His apostles, the Holy Spirit—the power behind *all* signs and wonders—gave "gifts [or, distributions]" to certain believers for the purpose of confirming that the things being taught and done in Christ's church were in fact approved by God (2:4).

The Law of Moses was from heaven, being ordained by angels; the gospel is also from heaven but is ordained by the Son of God. The gospel, then, supersedes whatever had gone before it since Christ supersedes every angel in heaven. By implication, this also means that those seeking God cannot pursue anything *less* than the gospel of God's Son.

Questions

1.) What does the fact that we are in the "last days" imply concerning:

    a.   our placement in the scheme of *all* of God's "times or epochs" (Acts 1:7)?

    b.   the sequence of God's revelation to man?

    c.   any future messiahs, prophets, or lawgivers?

2.) Why is it necessary to establish the fact of Christ's supremacy over angels? (Consider Gal. 1:8, 2 Peter 2:4, and Jude 1:6 and 1:9 in your answer.)

3.) "With privilege comes responsibility" is an old adage. If today we are more privileged to receive a much better message given to us by a much greater Prophet than what Israel received, then are we to be *more* responsible than the ancient Israelites or *less*? Please explain.

4.) God has not just given us a *message* (gospel) to believe but also a *reason to believe it.* Given this passage (2:1–4), what are some reasons to believe, and why are these necessary to accompany the message itself?

Lesson Two:
Christ's Supremacy over Humankind
(2:5–18)

God Subjected the Earth to Men (2:5–8): Having established that Christ has supremacy over all angels, the writer now turns his attention to His relationship with humankind. His use of "world" here (in 2:5) means literally "the inhabited earth"; "to come" refers to that age after the word of God was communicated by angels (Heb 2:2).[17] Thus, the writer simply means: "the Christian age," for it is this of "which we are speaking." In other words, while angels were used to communicate to men in the ancient world, the "world to come" (in comparison to the ancient world) is overseen by Christ, even though the physical world was put in subjection to people, not angels.

The quote from Psalm 8:4–6 (in 2:6–7) does not speak of Christ, as many assume, but of mortal men. Human beings are "for a little while lower than the angels" in *glory* and *proximity* to God (2:6–8).[18] While angels now behold the face of God (Luke 1:19, Mat. 18:10), we have no such privilege. We have received "glory and honor" in an earthly context but not in full. Nonetheless, the gospel promises that people will also receive dominion over the future world with Christ (Mat. 19:28–29, Rev. 3:21, etc.). At that time, believers will reign *over* angels (1 Cor. 6:2–3). The "all things in subjection under his [man's] feet" phrase recalls 1:13, in which Jesus' enemies will acknowledge their subjection to Him.

In the beginning, God put the entire earth in subjection to human beings (Gen. 1:29–30, 9:1–3, Isa. 45:18, etc.). When Adam sinned, he brought a curse upon himself that negatively affected his (and his posterity's) relationship with the earth (Gen. 3:17–19). In other words, things are not *now* as God originally intended. "We do not yet see all things subjected to him [man]" (2:8b)—that is, the physical, earthly system has not yet been fulfilled, and the future realm has not yet been visibly disclosed to us. Man was made to be a master of this world but instead made himself a slave to sin (Gen. 4:7, John 8:34, Rom. 6:16, etc.), and the natural world suffers because of it.

Jesus Also Was Made "Lower than the Angels" (2:9–18): While we do not yet see in ourselves or our world the full scope of what God had intended for us, in Christ we *do* see this (2:9). Because of the perfect life He led upon this earth, He now has been "crowned with glory and honor" in heaven (Phil. 2:9). While He was on earth (John 1:14), He was "for a little while lower than the angels" to identify with and thus intercede for us. Yet, even in that state, angels ministered *to* Jesus but never wielded authority *over* Him. Thus, in His case, "lower than the angels" has to do with His human nature, not His divine nature: He became human without ceasing to be the divine Son of God.

Jesus and His Brethren (2:9–18): As a man, Jesus could not have descended any lower than His death upon the cross. That He "[tasted] death" for everyone (2:9) does not mean merely that Jesus died, for every person "tastes death" in that sense. But for the Son of God to "taste death" implies the *full importance* of His sacrificial death: what it signified, what it accomplished, what it overcame. The author implies rhetorically: What (other) man has accomplished this? What angel? What *law*?

The Law of Moses, though ordained by angels and ratified by animal blood, was still unable to do what Christ accomplished through His death (2:10–13). The Creator gave Himself up for His Creation; nothing *less* than this kind of sacrifice could have atoned for the sin *of* the Creation. Christ made *Himself* the "author" [lit., leader; captain] of salvation through His own suffering. He was "perfected" through His offering in that His sufferings fulfilled the objective of God's plan of redemption for man (for example, Isa. 53:10 and Col. 1:19–20). Through His sufferings, "many sons" (i.e., faithful believers) are saved. He is the "author of salvation" in that He defines the terms of His saving gospel, just as He defines the faith God requires of those saved by it (Heb. 12:2).

Since Christ has so identified with man, even having endured unspeakable suffering for our sake, "He is not ashamed to call them [believers] brethren" (2:11). Christ the Sanctifier and those who are sanctified are all from one Father: we are made sons of God through Him (Gal. 3:26–27).[19] As God's only begotten Son, Christ is our Brother as well as our Lord: He identifies with us intimately and compassionately.

Jesus so completely identifies with us that He became "flesh and blood" as we are (2:14–16). The *purpose* for this was to rescue "the children" (i.e., faithful believers) from the grip of fear and death (Col. 1:12–14). "The only way He could deal with death was by dying, and the only way He could die was by becoming human."[20] As Christ and "His brethren" have a common existence (in the flesh), so we have a common enemy: Satan.[21] As Jesus defeated Satan's power over death, so we defeat Satan's power over our (spiritual) death; as Jesus overcame Satan, so we overcome him (Mat. 12:29, John 16:33).[22]

The "slavery" mentioned here (2:15) is the insurmountable burden of trying to achieve righteousness through law-keeping or any human effort (Gal. 5:1–4). It is the *pronouncement* of death and *anticipation* of punishment for having sinned against God. Satan has no authority to cast souls into hell, but he has long accused sinners of being unworthy of God's atonement. He induces people to sin, incapacitates them with guilt, and capitalizes on their fear of judgment. He deceives sinners into believing they can achieve righteousness apart from God's grace.[23]

Yet Christ has removed all Satan's threats: His blood cleanses believers from all sin (1 John 1:7) and therefore spares us from the punishment for sin. Once enlightened with divine truth, we no longer are to be seduced by Satan's deceptions. Christ offers no salvation to angels but only to "His brethren" (2:16).[24] The "descendant of Abraham" refers to the children of God (Rom. 4:22–24, Gal. 3:6–9, and 3:26–29).

To become our "merciful and faithful high priest," Christ had to personally identify with those for whom He intercedes (2:17–18). The high priest's primary responsibility was to minister to the "things pertaining to God," and especially in making "propitiation" for sinners.[25] "Propitiation" is the act of appeasing God's wrath through blood sacrifice; it seeks God's mercy in the place of His judgment.[26] This is the first direct mention of Jesus' high-priestly role, yet this subject will be discussed throughout much of this epistle from here forward.[27]

Christ's blood covers sins as a demonstration of mercy toward sinners. He does not merely hide our sins or forgive them in anticipation of some (yet) future action. Rather, He *properly removes them once for all.* While this was impossible under the Law of Moses, the Levitical sacrificial system foreshadowed it. Christ provided what was lacking in that system—the *uncorrupted blood of a perfect human specimen who was also a divine being*—and thus absolutely fulfilled the requirement *of* law in His own offering (Rom. 8:1–4).[28]

Christ was *tempted*, yet without sin (2:18; see Heb. 4:15). He faced what we face, but He did not succumb to that to which we have succumbed— the lies, delusion, and seduction of Satan's enticement to exalt and/ or gratify ourselves. To be *like* His "brethren," He had to endure what they endure; to *intercede* for His brethren (as their Redeemer), He had to overcome that which had overcome them. Jesus was "tempted in what He has suffered," which means He bore sufferings as part of His temptation: He had the ability to forego these sufferings, but He accepted them instead (see Mat. 26:53).

Questions

1.) We know that the physical world suffers under the curse that God placed upon it because of man's sin (2:8). Do Christians also continue to live under this curse, even though they are in Christ? (Consider Rom. 8:18–23 and 2 Cor. 4:16–18 in your answer.)

2.) Why is it "fitting" (or appropriate) for Christ to suffer to the extent that He did (2:10)? When Christians suffer for their faith in Him, is this also "fitting"? Please explain. (Consider Rom. 8:16–17, 2 Tim. 1:8–12, and 1 Peter 3:13–16 in your answer.)

3.) If Jesus has successfully defeated Satan, then why does he still exert so much influence and power over so many Christians, overwhelming and imprisoning them?

   a. Is it because Satan is not *truly* defeated?

   b. Or is it because we are still slaves to the "fear of death" after all?

   c. Or is it a matter of "unbelief" on the part of those Christians?

SECTION TWO:
WARNINGS AGAINST APOSTASY
(3:1—6:20)

Lesson Three:
First Warning against Apostasy
(3:1–19)

Given all that he has presented so far, the writer asks his readers to "consider" Jesus as "the Apostle and High Priest of our confession" (3:1)—really, to dwell deeply on who He is. There have been several apostles, but Jesus was the ideal Apostle (recall 1:1–2). There are many shepherds in the brotherhood, but Jesus is the Chief Shepherd (1 Peter 5:4). The Jews had numerous high priests over the centuries, but Jesus is a greater priest than all of them. Our "confession" (in this context) acknowledges His supremacy over all other lords or saviors (see 1 Tim. 6:12–13).

Christ's Superiority over Moses (3:2–6): While similarities do exist between the two men, Jesus Christ was far superior to Moses in all things. Moses was a *servant* of God, but Christ is the *Son* of God; Moses served *in* God's "house" but Christ rules *over* it. Furthermore, Moses *belongs* to God's "house" but Christ *is the house*, in essence (3:6; see Col. 1:18, 1 Tim. 3:15, and 1 Peter 2:4–5). "We should not think of two houses, the Old Testament and the New Testament house; these are but one house that is composed of God's spiritual people."[29]

Christians are members of God's household only "if we hold fast our confidence" (3:6). Our membership, fellowship, and salvation are conditioned upon our continued faithfulness to the One who provides these things. The writer is thus warning those who are considering abandoning their allegiance to Christ as their Lord. "These Hebrew

Christians had confessed Jesus as their Apostle and High Priest. They do not begin to understand what Jesus is and means if they are tempted to give him up."[30]

The Exodus as an Allegory (3:7–11): Even though Christ is the head of God's "house," we only benefit from this when we put *confidence* (obedient faith) in Him until the very end (3:7; see Heb. 10:23). To support his argument, the writer cites Psalm 95:7–11, a psalm of David. This quote refers to the first generation of Israel that God led out of Egyptian captivity and repeatedly refused to be faithful to Him. They "tested" God (i.e., tried His patience with their doubt and complaining) to the point where God refused to give them what He had originally promised them, since this promise was conditioned upon their faithfulness to Him (Num. 14:11, 22, 1 Cor. 10:1–5).

To "harden your hearts" means to be insensitive and unresponsive toward God's commands. Because the Israelites disbelieved His ability to perform, the entire generation (save for two men, Joshua and Caleb) was condemned to die in the wilderness instead of entering the Promised Land (Canaan).

Just as the Israelites lost their lives for unbelief, a Christian can lose his soul for *his* unbelief (3:12). Just as those Israelites were denied the Promised Land, an unbelieving Christian will be denied entrance into the kingdom of God. An "evil, unbelieving heart" does not have to commit acts of blatant wickedness: he only needs to recant his profession of faith in Christ. Unbelief does not mean failing to believe in God at all but resisting His word and His will in any sense. All resistance is unbelief; all unbelief is a form of resistance. On the other hand, one will remain a partaker of Christ who continues to "hold fast" his faith in Him (3:14; see Col. 1:21–23 and Rev. 2:10).

The urgent message here (in 3:13) is, in essence, "Respond to His voice *while there is still time to do so!*" Likewise, we are instructed to "encourage one another" to prevent such evil and unbelief from taking root in any Christian's heart (see Heb. 10:23–25)—while looking to ourselves as well (Gal. 6:1–2). The "deceitfulness of sin" will harden a person's heart (i.e., make him insensitive to God's grace) so that he will no longer listen to Christ's voice.

The writer then poses three rhetorical questions, based upon Psalm 95, to underscore his message (3:16–18):

1. Did Israel provoke God with their unbelief?—*yes, and they suffered disastrous consequences as a result.*
2. Was God angry with those people's unbelief?—*yes, to the point that He cursed them to die in the wilderness rather than enter the "rest" He had appointed for them.*
3. Did God swear that these disobedient people would not enter the Promised Land?—*yes, and [implied] you will not enter heaven, if you also practice unbelief.*

"So we see that they were not able to enter because of unbelief" (3:19). This is the essential point: unbelief is not only a sin but is ruinous to the one who practices it. The Jewish Christians who were contemplating abandoning their faith in Christ were in danger of becoming *unbelievers,* even if they devoted themselves to Moses and Aaron. Likewise, Christians who turn away from Christ make themselves *unbelievers,* regardless of what or whom they turn to instead—even if it is done with good intentions or in the name of God.

Questions

1.) The premise of *Hebrews* is to warn Jewish Christians from abandoning what they have in Christ in pursuit of what they left behind under the Law of Moses. Would this abandonment be considered an act of rebellion against God or is He permissive to allow people to worship Him in whatever way they choose?

2.) Saving grace is, in essence, everything God does for us that we cannot do for ourselves regarding salvation.[31]

    a. Given this, why does resistance of God's saving grace always imply self-righteousness and self-reliance?

    b. How does the practice of *these* (self-righteousness and self-reliance) translate to "unbelief" and a "hardness of heart"?

3.) Based upon the example of Israel, is God's saving grace unconditional? How long does His mercy last? How long will He tolerate one's unbelief? (Consider Rom. 2:4, 11:22, 2 Peter 3:9 and 3:14–15 in your answer.)

Lesson Four:
Danger of Forfeiting
What Was Promised
(4:1–16)

The Need for Faith (4:1–2): In this passage (4:1–13), the writer gives a second warning against apostasy [lit., turning away from the truth]. One's salvation is a profound responsibility; the God of salvation is to be regarded with utmost reverence. Thus, "let us fear" (4:1)—let us regard Him in a healthy, respectful, and obedient manner (Phil. 2:12). God's promise of rest to the believer is conditioned upon that person's faithfulness to His covenant. In other words, the promise itself is not in question or prone to fail; rather, one's personal belief *in* that promise is the only variable.

As a historical case in point, ancient Israel had "good news" [lit., gospel] preached to them, but they did not put faith in it (4:2). "They" refers to the Israelites who had come out of Egypt, passed through the Red Sea, and observed many signs and wonders. God had given them every reason to believe in His ability to perform, yet they chronically persisted in unbelief. This culminated in their refusal to believe that God could bring them into the Promised Land (4:3–5). Likewise, we (Christians) have had the gospel preached to us, and we have believed it. Yet if we do not continue *in* belief, then this good news will be of no benefit to us. In that case, the gospel which was meant to save us will instead condemn us (Rom. 11:22).

God's "Rest" for Believers (4:3–11): The writer ties God's "rest" (from His work of the Creation—Gen. 2:1–3) with the "rest" He promises to Christians (4:3–11). God could only "rest" from this work because He finished it.[32] However, our work (discipleship to Christ) remains unfinished, so we cannot yet "rest" from it. The writer here touches on a profound point: the "rest" that follows a completed work is itself a part *of* that work. The two actions—working and resting—go together: one's work anticipates a "rest" from it, and one's "rest" implies that the work which he performed is in fact finished.[33] Once we complete our ministry to Christ on earth, we will enter God's rest that He now enjoys having completed *His* work of Creation.

However, if one fails to complete his work (due to his unbelief), he forfeits the rest God had promised him. God has provided the *time* for responding to this "good news": it is "today"—and God promises no one a tomorrow (4:6–7; see James 4:13–17). This is true for the backsliding Christian as it is for one who remains outside of Christ. In a parallel thought, God promised Israel rest from their enemies in Canaan as long as they remained faithful to Him (4:8; see Deut. 12:10). Yet Joshua never gave to Israel the kind of rest that Christ offers us: theirs was physical (an inheritance of land); ours is spiritual (an eternal home in God's kingdom). To enjoy this spiritual rest, one must respond *now* ("today") while the window of opportunity still exists; otherwise, he may forfeit this opportunity altogether.[34]

A "Sabbath rest" (4:9) indicates the *kind* of rest of which the writer speaks. God imposed a Sabbath rest upon Israel in honor of His own rest from the work of Creation (Exod. 20:8–11). This rest (day) was observed at the end of every week, as the final part of the entire cycle of a seven-day period. (Note: the "rest" was *part* of the full week, not separate from it.) In the spiritual context, a "Sabbath rest" indicates the completion of *all* the believer's earthly work in the Lord (Eph. 2:10) since he will have entered God's "rest" forever (4:10). Unlike what Israel faced, there will be no *new* cycle (a new week) beginning after this since one's life here on earth will then be finished forever.

"Therefore let us be diligent to enter that rest … " (4:11). "Diligence" involves earnest endeavor, applied effort, and a sense of urgency (as in Rom. 12:10–11 and 2 Peter 1:5). The believer is admonished to exert himself productively in anticipation of his "rest" with the Lord. Entrance into the eternal kingdom is not easy (Acts 14:22) and we must "Strive to enter" it (Luke 13:24).

The Discerning Word of God (4:12–13): In any case, God knows the true disposition of every heart (4:12–13). One cannot feign "belief" any more than he can hide his sins. God sees every object, person, and soul; nothing escapes His notice, not even what is (to us) invisible, indiscernible, and imperceptible. The "word" does not define exactly what the human "soul" or "spirit" is, but it is capable of *dividing* (or making a distinction between) the two. The natural sense of "joints and marrow" is used figuratively "to denote the inmost essence of man's spiritual nature,"[35] referring to that part of human life invisible to the human eye (and even the human heart) but fully revealed to God.

The "word of God" here is not the literal Bible since words on pages are neither living nor active. It is also not Christ, in this context: the writer never refers to Him as "the word of God" but instead as "the Son of God" (see 4:14). In the present context, "word of God" refers to the dynamic and convicting *power* and *omniscience* of God's Spirit (as in John 16:8–11, which speaks of the work of the Spirit among men; see also 1 Peter 1:23–25). God's commandments—their power and their convicting and transforming effect—is elsewhere called "the sword of the Spirit" (Eph. 6:17), which parallels the present passage. It is the Spirit that both reveals and convicts the human heart. The Bible is the written record of *what* the Spirit does but not *how* He does it.[36]

Questions

1.) Based on the example of ancient Israel (4:2), does everyone today who hears the gospel—even on a regular basis—automatically exercise faith in it? If not, why not?

2.) All *members* of Christ's body have "work" to do and should be busy doing it. But, despite the stern warning presented here (4:1–11) against *failing* to "work," some Christians remain unmotivated.

    a.   Given the present passage, what *ought* to motivate a Christian into fulfilling his personal ministry to God, whatever that ministry (or ministries) might be?

    b.   What *interferes* with this motivation—and how can a person remove that interference?

3.) God's examination of the human soul, through the agency of His Son (as High Priest) and His Spirit (as the "sword" that pierces the innermost part of us) is parallel to the ancient Levitical system. Under the Law of Moses, animals brought *to* the priests for sacrifice had to be thoroughly examined *by* the priests (Lev. 22:17–33). Only unblemished animals were fit (or appropriate) for sacrifice; likewise, only faithful believers are fit to approach the throne of God.

    a.   Given this, can any person come to God on his own terms, according to a self-determined belief system, or in any manner of his own choosing?

    b.   What if someone fails the examination, so to speak—will God allow him to have fellowship with Him *anyway*?

Lesson Five:
Christ as Our High Priest
(4:14—5:10)

Approaching the Throne of Grace (4:14–16): The believer does not have to fear the scrutiny of an all-seeing God on his own since Jesus—"a great high priest"—advocates and mediates for him (4:14–16). Instead of merely passing through a veil into the innermost sanctuary of the temple, as a Levitical high priest would have done, Jesus came before the actual Presence of God. Thus, Jesus serves two roles: He is both *King* and *High Priest* of God's kingdom (as prophesied in Zech. 6:11–13). No high priest of Israel ever sat on a throne; no king of Israel ever ministered as a high priest. Priests mediate, kings rule; priests work standing up (at the altar), kings work sitting down (upon a throne).

Christians are to approach Christ's "throne of grace" with *confidence*, which can only be gained if we "hold fast [or, cling tightly to] our confession." This confession (here) alludes to our original commitment to Christ (1 Tim. 6:12–13). As our High Priest, Christ does not merely act in an official capacity, carrying out the rites and functions expected of one in such a position, but is *personally aware* of our struggles and can *identify* with "our weaknesses" (i.e., of being human).

In our presentation before Christ (through prayer), we "receive mercy" and "find grace" (4:16). "Mercy" or compassion is the withholding of what is deserved (as punishment); "grace" is whatever is undeserved or unearned (as a gift). Christ's "throne of grace" symbolizes His all-sufficient atonement (or high-priestly work) <u>and</u> all-sufficient authority (or kingly work): the first work *makes* us worthy; the second *pronounces* us worthy.

A Comparison of the Priesthoods (5:1–10): The earthly high priests of the Levitical order—namely, Aaron and his sons—were adequate for their time but had insurmountable limitations. They were "taken from among men" (5:1)—i.e., they could act on behalf of men but could not overcome their own human deficiencies. Even so, the high priests stood (in a sense) between God and men. To God, they offered gifts and sacrifices; to men, they offered intercession to God and pardon for men's offenses. The priests dealt with (spiritually) "ignorant and misguided" people (5:2), yet they were constantly aware of their own imperfections since they had to make sacrifices for their own sins before ministering to the needs of others (Lev. 16:6).

As important as his role was, Aaron (or his successors) never declared himself a high priest apart from being "called by God" (5:4). God ordained his priesthood (through the Law of Moses), not men. This is significant because it shows his priesthood as being *subservient* to the Law rather than being *transcendent* of it (as in the case of Christ). Christ also did not appoint Himself a priest, but His priesthood was conferred upon Him by God (5:5–6). Aaron's appointment was through the Law; Christ's was through a divine oath (see Heb. 7:20–21). Just as God declared Christ as King, so He declared Him to be "a priest forever." Both facts are confirmed by prophecies (Psalm 2:7 and 110:4).

To serve as a High Priest, Christ had to prove His obedience to the Father. In 5:7–8, the writer alludes to Jesus' anguished prayer in the garden of Gethsemane, just prior to His arrest (Mat. 26:36–46). While it may appear that Jesus prayed *not to die*, the real essence of His prayer is that *His Father's will be done*, regardless of the cost. This surrender to the Father's will is the "piety" (i.e., reverence, godly fear, or religious devotion) to which the writer refers. Thus, Jesus' work as our High Priest began on earth *in anticipation* of it being fully realized in heaven.

On the other hand, Jesus did not "learn" obedience like we do—through trial and error; through resistance (first) then submission (ultimately) (5:8). It was not that He had to be taught *how* to obey; rather, He had to "learn" to *experience* obedience in the flesh even through immense suffering. Through perfect obedience, He became "the source [or, author] of eternal salvation" (5:9) for all those who also are striving to be obedient to God—not with Jesus' same flawlessness *but* sharing His attitude of submission (John 8:29 and 1 Peter 2:21–22).

In proving Himself worthy for the office, Jesus was declared (or, designated; ordained) by God "as a high priest forever according to the order of Melchizedek" (5:10), a reference to the king-priest of Salem whom Abraham encountered after his battle with the kings of the east (Gen. 14). Thus, Jesus' priesthood is based upon the dual office (the "order") of Melchizedek, even while fulfilling the symbolic forms prefigured in the Levitical priesthood. Even so, as significant as the roles of Melchizedek and the Aaronic priesthood were, no man could secure "eternal salvation" for *anyone*—including himself—except for Jesus Christ.

Questions

1.) On what occasions might a Christian be "in time of need" of Christ's mercy and grace (4:14–16)? If a person refuses to go to Christ for help in such times, would this be considered a resistance of God's grace? Please explain.

2.) The Levitical high priests (Aaron and his descendants) held the highest religious office in all Israel yet could not rise above the inadequacies of those whom they served. This pointed forward to a *perfection* of their role since it was incomplete by itself.

    a.   How did *Christ* rise above these inadequacies? Is He the perfect High Priest?

    b.   Will there ever be another priest that parallels or even supersedes that of the high priesthood of Christ? Why or why not?

3.) Aaron did not make himself a high priest; God designated him for this office (5:4). How does this same principle apply when determining whether one becomes a *Christian*? Does he appoint himself or does God appoint Him?

Lesson Six:
Second Warning against Apostasy
(5:11—6:20)

The Danger of Dullness of Hearing: The *Hebrews* writer has thus far expounded upon Christ's superiority to angels, humankind, Moses, and Aaron. Yet all this is lost upon those whose senses are dulled with mediocre (spiritual) education and whose hearts are laced with doubt (5:11). The original recipients of this letter should have been much more grounded than they were; they ought to have been *defending* and *imitating* Christ rather than contemplating their abandonment of Him. Yet distraction, disinterest, fear, lack of diligence, and inadequate preparation on their part had left them soft, unfocused, and undisciplined—thus, they were gullible, weak, and seeking the path of least resistance.

Deliberate immaturity—through lack of desire, effort, and growth—is never acceptable to God (5:12–13). Those who have been Christians long enough to take on the responsibilities of teachers, but remain forever students or even bystanders, will never learn to appreciate Christ's work, priesthood, or salvation.[37] Like an adult who must be nourished again as though a young child, so is the backward and dysfunctional condition of one who, despite all the advantages provided for him, reverts to an infantile spiritual life (1 Cor. 13:11). Instead of moving forward, he is stuck on "elementary principles."

"But solid food is for the mature" (5:14)—this refers to what a person can *swallow*: the "infant" believer, only milk; the mature believer, meat and solid food (1 Cor. 3:1–2). The mature Christian is "trained" to discriminate or judge between what is to be believed (or useful) and what is not (or useless). The writer's original reading audience, in failing to appreciate the united offices of Christ's kingship and priesthood, are not showing mature discernment.

Every believer must begin with elementary teachings of Christ and learn them well (6:1–3). Yet, *having* learned such teachings, one is expected to grow beyond them. Once we have been grounded in the foundational teachings (like repentance, faith toward God, baptism, etc.), we are expected to advance beyond these.[38] This does not mean we can never re-visit subjects we have once learned; it means we should not permanently *camp* on them, and even in revisiting them we should do so with greater understanding.

The Peril of Unbelief (6:4–8): This next passage (6:4–8) is one of the most unsettling of this entire epistle. Perhaps preachers and teachers have watered down these words with assurances that, no matter how many times a Christian "falls away," he can always come back. While in some cases this may be true (depending on how one defines "falls away"), in other cases this may *not* be true.

If any passage in the NT confirms the possibility of a Christian losing his soul, this is it. This (6:4–6) does not describe a person who *thought* he was a Christian yet was mistaken. It describes a person who had indeed *become* a child of God, then turned his back on such sonship and privilege. Upon his having "fallen away," his restoration is "impossible"; in this case, he cannot be renewed merely with "repentance." If a person does not respond to the gospel after having already received it, nothing else can be done for him. His heart is so callous that not even the greatest events in all history and the universe—namely, that God "in the flesh" died for his sins and then rose from the dead—will affect him. Not only is he overcome with sin, but he has forfeited the opportunity to escape his demise.

To fall away is to "crucify" to oneself (i.e., in his own heart; by his own actions). This identifies him with those who nailed Jesus to the cross. The difference here is that those who crucified Jesus did so largely in ignorance (see Luke 23:34 and 1 Cor. 2:6–8). This person, however, is not acting in ignorance but in sheer defiance, treason, and unbelief, being wholly unconcerned for the price that was paid for his forgiveness

(2 Peter 1:9). He has received the blessing of salvation ("the rain") but his heart remains barren, lifeless, and unfruitful (6:7–8). He brings upon himself a divine curse (see John 15:1–6 for comparison).

Recollections of Former Deeds and Enthusiasm (6:9–12): Despite the strong language of the last several verses, the writer tones down his message now (6:9), as if to say, "While you are in danger, not all is lost *yet*." The Hebrew Christians have not yet gone down the road of apostasy; there remains opportunity to repent. And God is not unjust (or unrighteous) to overlook all that has already been done in His honor (6:10). The writer's implied question to his readers is: will *you* be unjust by turning your back upon all *He* has done for *you*? Diligence of faith is required on their part; without such diligence, believers become "sluggish"—lazy, lethargic, dull of thinking, and unmotivated. On the other hand, if they remain steadfast in hope, they will follow in the footsteps of those who have *already inherited* the promises (6:11–12).

The Steadfast Anchor of God's Promise (6:13–20): While much has been said in Scripture about Abraham's faithfulness to God, here the writer emphasizes God's faithfulness to Abraham (6:13). It is true that Abraham "patiently waited" *twenty-five years* for his "hope" (Isaac, the son of promise) to be realized (6:14–15). Yet, it was God who made this hope possible against all human effort and ability (Rom. 4:16–22). In His promise to Abraham, God "swore by Himself": He invoked His own holy Name as a guarantee of that promise. This means that if God had *failed* to keep His promise, He would have violated His own divine nature.

Since this is an impossible thing to do—for God to be unfaithful, deny Himself, or lie (2 Tim. 2:13, Titus 1:2)—He provides absolute assurance to the one to whom the promise is made. An "oath" is not just a spoken promise but carries with it the binding force of the thing or authority by which it is sworn. Men swear by an authority greater than themselves, but God must swear by His own Name, since there is no greater name or authority. Thus, we see "two unchangeable things": first, God's unalterable divine nature; second, His oath (promise) which is supported by that divine nature (6:16–18).

Just as Abraham hoped in a God who cannot lie, fail, or be bound by human limitations, so Christians are to hope in this same God. Jesus Christ is the realization of that hope: in Him we have "taken refuge" (6:18).[39] We can take "strong encouragement" in who Christ is, what He has accomplished, and how He can help us. The believer has *stability* and a *connection* to something immovable despite the storms of life, trials of faith, etc., just like a ship being held fast by its anchor despite the tempest (6:19–20).

But the Hebrew Christians, not much a seafaring people, would more readily identify with One who enters "within the veil," that is, as a high priest (see Lev. 16:11–14). Thus, our hope is securely embedded in the One who has entered within the *heavenly* veil already, "as a forerunner for us." For now, just as the anchor on the bottom of the ocean is invisible to the sailor, so Christ in heaven is (so far) invisible to the believer—but this will not always be the case.

Having admonished his readers for their lax attention, the writer will resume where he left off in speaking of Melchizedek, and especially of the high priesthood of Christ (in chapter 7).

Questions

1.) There is no question that 5:11–14 applies to some in the church today. The real question is: how can we convince such people that what they are doing not only contradicts their professed beliefs but also threatens their eternity? How does the *Hebrews* writer handle this?

2.) What causes a Christian to reject what he once so strongly claimed to believe in (6:4–8)? (There may be several answers.)

    a.   What does this say about the satanic power of *unbelief*?

    b.   How does this underscore the constant need to actively *nurture* one's faith (see 2 Peter 1:5–11) rather than putting it on cruise control, so to speak?

3.) In 6:11, the writer admonishes Christians to show "diligence" in their faith. What is "diligence"? Why is this necessary for faith to become healthy and growing? What does the *lack* of diligence always lead to?

4.) Aaron, though a high priest, was *never* referred to as a "forerunner" for us. Why is this? How is it that Christ, our eternal High Priest, *is* a "forerunner" for us (6:20)?

SECTION THREE:
A NEW PRIESTHOOD AND COVENANT
(7:1—10:18)

Lesson Seven:
The New Priesthood Not Based on Law
(7:1–22)

W e do not know anything about Melchizedek than what is written in Gen. 14:18–20 and here (7:1–3). Not everyone believes that he was even an actual person. Regardless, Scripture presents Melchizedek as a real, flesh-and-blood, historical person, in the same context as Abraham and King Chedorlaomer (whom Abraham fought against and defeated). This is what we know of him:

- ❑ He was a king of Salem, likely the city-state of what was later known as Jerusalem.
- ❑ He was a priest of Most High God, though he lived some 500 years before the Levitical priesthood.
- ❑ He met Abraham (then, still "Abram") after his victory in battle and blessed him.
- ❑ He received from Abraham "a tenth part of all the spoils"[40] that Abraham gained through his victory over the kings of the east.
- ❑ His name means "king of righteousness."
- ❑ Since Salem (his domain) means "peace," he was also known as "king of peace."
- ❑ He was "without father, without mother, without genealogy"—while some take this literally, it is meant figuratively: he descended from no chosen ancestry or dynasty (like Aaron did, being a descendent of Levi).

- He had "neither beginning of days nor end of life"—again, figuratively-speaking, his age is not recorded, nor his birth or death; compare this to the patriarchs in Genesis. It was *as though* he simply appeared out of nowhere, received tithes from Abraham, and then retreated into obscurity, beyond the record of human history.
- He was "made like the Son of God"—not *being* the Son, but his office foreshadows that *of* the Son; in a sense, he was a *type* of "Son of God" yet to come.
- He "remains a priest perpetually"—that is, since there is no record of his beginning or end, his presence in history continues without closure, permanently sustained.
- He is neither an ordinary man nor a divine figure; he is mysterious, unknown, unprecedented, and unexpected.

Abraham was a great man, to be sure, but even he paid tithes to Melchizedek (7:4). Abraham was great because of his faith and covenant relationship with God; Melchizedek, because of his position as a king *and* a high priest of God. A "tenth" [lit., tithe] represents an honorable representation of one's income or gain. Centuries later, Levites were to receive a tenth of every Israelite's income per the Law of Moses; a tenth of the Levite's own income was given to the priests themselves (7:5; see Num. 18:21, 24–26).

But Levites were descendants of Abraham; they were "in the system," so to speak, while Melchizedek had no ancestral ties to Abraham. The idea being strongly presented here is that, because of this, Melchizedek stood *above* Abraham in rank, which is why Abraham gave him anything (7:6–7). Melchizedek was a mortal man (7:8), but his office—its concept, symbolism, and foreshadow of that which was to come—remains forever fixed ("lives on") in time and history.[41]

Since Abraham paid tithes to Melchizedek, then Levi (through Abraham) also paid tithes to him, and whatever priesthood is derived *through* Abraham (i.e., the Levitical priesthood) is also subordinate to Melchizedek's (7:9–10).[42] Thus, the dual-office nature of Melchizedek is greater than that of Levi and the priesthood bestowed upon his descendants. And Christ, though His priesthood follows the "order" of Melchizedek, was infinitely greater than Melchizedek himself.

The fact that God made Christ a High Priest of a new order necessarily implies the inadequacy of the first (Levitical) priesthood (7:11). And since it was a law given to humans that creates human priests, a change in priesthood *necessarily demands* a change in law also (7:12). These two things (priesthood and law) cannot be separated: if one changes, so must the other. To underscore his point, the writer reminds his readers that Jesus did not descend from Levi but was from the tribe of Judah. Even so, God declared Him to be "a great high priest" (recall 4:14), but not a Levitical priest. Jesus could not minister to the physical temple or offer sacrifices on its altar (7:13–14).

The two priesthoods, both being from God, cannot coexist for the same people (the Jews); the former must cease so that the latter may begin. In perfectly fulfilling the Law to which the priests ministered, Christ also made obsolete the function of its priesthood: all that the Law foreshadowed and prophesied (in its oracles and types) was summed up in Him (Eph. 1:9–10). The objective having been fulfilled by Christ for the Law *and* its priests meant that they were no longer needed (Mat. 5:17). Those who would abandon Christ for the Law of Moses would be attempting to resurrect a system that God Himself had ended.[43]

Melchizedek's priesthood was not based on Abraham's lineage or the Law of Moses. It was already in existence when Abraham met him; Abraham had nothing to do with it. The "indestructible life" (7:15–16) refers to the timelessness and (human) incorruption of Melchizedek's priesthood. This does not refer to Melchizedek himself but the symbolic character and dual function of his office. Jesus did not resume Melchizedek's literal position but entered one *on the order* of it, according to its *likeness*. While Melchizedek's "life" (ministry) is indestructible in *type*, Jesus' life is *in fact* indestructible since He lives forever. Thus, Jesus brought to spiritual completion what Melchizedek's office could only foreshadow in a physical capacity (7:17).

The "former commandment" (i.e., Law of Moses) was "set aside" due to its "weakness" (7:18): it simply could not and was never *intended* to do what Christ alone accomplished. The Law was "weak" in that it was *unable* to remove sin (Acts 13:38–39, Rom. 8:3, and Heb. 10:4). It was rendered useless (or obsolete) in that it has been fulfilled by Christ and thus superseded by a superior system of atonement *in* Christ. The Law, though ideal for its intended use, could not produce perfect men or a perfect priesthood (7:19).

Christ's Divine Ordination (7:20–22): God has ordained His Son as an eternal High Priest with a divine oath or decree, not according to instructions and regulations set forth in a law given to men (7:20–21).[44] The supremacy of Christ's appointment means that He also becomes the "guarantee" (i.e., promise, assurance, or surety) of a "better covenant" (7:22). Since Jesus' priesthood has rendered both the Law and its priesthood obsolete, it is *necessarily implied* that the covenant God made with Israel has been fulfilled. Since it is fulfilled, it can no longer be workable or enforced; a "better covenant" has superseded it.[45]

Questions

1.) Throughout history, virtually every organized religion has required a priestly class to officiate over it. Why do religious people *need* priests? What would be necessarily implied if people (or their religion) did *not* need priests?

2.) Jesus belonged to a tribe (Judah) which had no right to officiate at the altar of the Mosaic tabernacle (7:13–14). What "altar" did Christ use to carry out His priestly ministry—or does He even have one (see Heb. 13:10–12)? Is an "altar" necessary for atonement? Please explain.

3.) How do we "draw near to God" (7:19) *differently* through Christ than the Israelites were able to do through their Law and its priesthood?

   a. Were they forgiven of their sins when they drew near to God just as we are forgiven when *we* draw near to Him? If so, why did we need a "better hope" and a "better covenant" (7:22)? If not, why not?

   b. If Jesus had never become our eternal High Priest, could *any* of us be saved, whether faithful Israelites or faithful Christians?

Lesson Eight:
Comparison of the Two Priesthoods
(7:23—8:13)

Christ's Superior Priesthood (7:24–28): Aaron's priesthood was finite, limited in scope, and transitional (7:23). It was never meant to be held forever by one mortal man, nor could it be summed up *in* one man. Yet Jesus' priesthood *is* summed up in one Man: Himself (7:24–25). Since He will not die, He has no heir-apparent, no replacement, and no successor. No one can terminate His office; no one can take away His life; He is unchangeable and indestructible (13:8). Since He forever *lives*, His priesthood will ever *endure*: He will always intercede for His people.

It was "fitting" [lit., suitable; proper; right[46]] for Christ to occupy the sublime role of an eternal High Priest (7:26–28). He is the ideal Person—indeed, the only *worthy* Person—who can fulfill every need of His people. He does not have the flaws, limitations, or moral inadequacies of the Levitical priests. He is a perfect Being; He is entirely innocent and cannot die or be destroyed. He identifies with sinners without having become one of them; thus, He does not need to offer sacrifices first for His sins before tending to ours. He does not minister here on earth but in the heavens. Everything about Him and His priesthood is superior to any person or earthly priesthood. His offering is "once for all"—a one-time, all-encompassing, and final blood offering for atonement of sin. There will be no other priest, priesthood, or blood offering.[47]

The Law, perfect as it was for the purpose it served, nonetheless appointed weak men to minister to it (7:28). Yet, God's divine oath has appointed an infinitely powerful, eternal, indestructible, and invincible High Priest "made perfect forever." *This* High Priest forgives people based upon His own authority and the perfect sacrifice of His own body and blood.

At the Right Hand of God (8:1–6): The writer does not merely say, "There *exists* such a High Priest," but that we *have* such a High Priest *actively interceding for all believers* (8:1). We have access to the "throne of grace" (recall 4:16) upon which sits the King and eternal High Priest—*our* King, *our* Priest! Aaron never reigned at the right hand of God, but merely served a primitive role as an earthly servant of God. Yet Jesus has "taken His seat" alongside the One who has given Him all power and glory (recall 1:3).

Christ serves in heaven, in the very Presence of the Father. This is vastly superior to any Levitical priest, who merely served a physical structure and ventured only once a year into the Holy of Holies, the innermost sanctuary of the tabernacle where the ark of the covenant was kept (8:2).[48] The "true tabernacle" is spiritual in nature; in essence, God Himself is the spiritual "tabernacle" (Rev. 21:22; see Heb. 9:11, 24).

A high priest who has no sacrifices or gifts to *offer* completely fails his responsibility as a *priest* (8:3–4). Likewise, Christ must have something to offer—something superior to whatever was offered under the Levitical system (since His office is superior to it). Indeed, He has offered that which no Levitical high priest could have possibly offered: His own uncorrupted life and sinless blood (Heb. 9:14). Likewise, earthly priests merely follow the patterns and instructions given them; otherwise, they would violate the very law that ordained them and to which they minister (8:5; see Exod. 25:9, 40, and Acts 7:44). These physical "copies" and "shadows" point forward to heavenly realities—something *outside* of themselves. Christ, however, is the *substance* or *reality*—i.e., that to which the shadows and types all alluded.

The writer summarizes his thoughts by reiterating the supremacy and majesty of Christ over all that has preceded Him (8:6):

- **"a more excellent ministry"**: a ministry superior to that of the Levitical priests in every way.
- **"mediator of a better covenant"**: superior to that which God made with Israel. That first covenant served as the basis for this new

covenant; it was necessary for the one to exist first to prepare men for what was to come.

❑ **"[a covenant] enacted on better promises"**: the "better promises" of the eternal covenant transcend the physical world and its concerns (Col. 3:1–4), since it deals primarily with the salvation of human souls.

Everything in Christ is "better" than all that preceded Him, "better" than anything else on earth. "Better" here does not mean merely better by comparison but *the best that there is*.

The New Covenant (8:7–13): A covenant is an agreement between two parties to form a relationship with mutually beneficial objectives. It is not merely a contract, which focuses only on a particular thing or work being performed but creates a relationship that did not previously exist. A covenant does at least two things. First, it defines the relationship itself through its wording and the description of the roles of the two (or more) parties coming together in agreement. Second, it gives life to the relationship, making it functional, productive, and mutually rewarding. In other words, things are now accomplished *because* of the relationship that could never be done *outside* (or in the absence) of it.

The only reason for God to make a covenant with people is to provide a means of fellowship that can overcome human sin. One who has never sinned against God does not need a covenant of salvation with Him.[49] God's covenants with people allows them to have fellowship with Him even though they have sinned against Him. There are provisions in the covenant that deal with past sins as well as those that will be committed in the future.

God's covenant with Israel (the two parties coming together in agreement) focused on the earthly concerns, such as family lineages (bloodlines), land inheritance, rightful dealings with fellow Israelites, ritual observances, festivals, etc. God's covenant with believers today is not a national covenant or even a group covenant: it establishes an agreement between Him and *each individual believer*—it is a very personal covenant and thus a very personal relationship. Upon our personal, individual agreement to God's covenant of salvation—culminating in our baptism—we are thus added to the sanctuary of all *other* believers who have already done the same thing (Acts 2:41, 47).

The first covenant was ideal for the situation at hand. The problem was not the covenant itself, but Israel (the "them" in 8:8) in that they were unable (and often unwilling) to keep it perfectly. Moreover, there was no means within the covenant itself to justify those who had violated it; this was its "fault" (or limitation). The covenant was perfect for that for which it was intended but looked *outside of itself* for its own completion. This completion came through the establishment of a "new covenant"—one that rests upon the perfect obedience of *Christ* (not us) and in which justification *is* possible.

The passage in 8:8–12 is quoted from Jer. 31:31–34.[50] God made a covenant with Israel based upon external laws, rituals, and regulations (Deut. 5:1–3) but they continually violated this agreement. Jeremiah, however, spoke of a future time when God would make a *new* covenant with Israel—*not* merely a recitation or reactivation of the *old* covenant, but a *better* (superior) one. Instead of focusing merely on external laws and regulations, this new covenant would be governed internally—i.e., through the indwelling of God's Holy Spirit (Rom. 8:9, 1 Cor. 6:19–20, Gal. 5:16, etc.).

From Jeremiah's day (6th century BC) to the time of Christ, the Jews followed and served under the *old* covenant, since the new one had not yet been revealed or put into effect. But in Jesus Christ, the new covenant is available to all people. This new covenant makes the old one obsolete; God does not offer two simultaneous (and competing) covenants to His people. The "days are coming" phrase OT language often refers to the messianic age (the reign of Messiah). This covenant would be "new" in:

❑ history (as an event).
❑ time (relative to the "old" or "first" covenant).

- people (all ethnicities are invited versus only Israelites; also, individual people are invited versus an entire nation).
- scope (eternal life versus earthly life).
- nature (spiritual realm versus physical realm).
- mediation (Jesus Christ versus mortal priests).
- ability (immediate forgiveness versus anticipation of a perfect sacrifice).
- terms, conditions, and stipulations (lifestyle, requirements, expectations, etc. revealed in the gospel versus those outlined in the Law of Moses).
- recording (on one's heart versus tablets of stone—Exod. 34:27–29, 2 Cor. 3:3).
- blood (of Jesus versus the blood of animals).
- blessings and curses (affecting one's eternity versus one's earthly circumstances or inheritance).

This new covenant would initially be offered to "the house of Israel and ... Judah" (8:8) but not exclusive to them. The "house of Israel/ Judah" does not speak of a renewed or reunified physical kingdom (as once existed under King David and Solomon), but a renewed *people* gathered in a completely new *context* (spiritual versus physical, political, or geographical). Since the Israelites did not keep their covenant (8:9– 10), God promised to bring about a new covenant that can be made to people of all nations and ethnicities.

This new covenant will not be written on stone (a reference to the stone tablets upon which the Ten Commandments were inscribed; see Deut. 10:1–2) but on the heart of every believer. This is not a new idea (Deut. 6:6) but is given new significance here. The expression "I will be their God, and they will be My people" is also not new,[51] but in Christ this is taken to an entirely new level. God's people will have a new identity— individually and collectively—through Christ.

In God's covenant with Christ, Israelite males were inducted into the covenant nation of Israel through circumcision on the "eighth day" (Lev. 12:2–3). Females had no physical identity with the covenant, and even the eight-day-old males had no clue what was happening. In other words, sons had to be taught over time what it meant to be an Israelite and were dependent upon their fathers to teach them (Deut. 6:7).

Now, however, people can learn the gospel anywhere, that is, from any person, at any place, in any nation, at any time (8:11). Anyone can "know the Lord," not only those whose fathers or families are already faithful. Also, women are included in the covenant as equal heirs (Gal. 3:28–29).[52] Thus, this new covenant transcends all the barriers imposed by the first covenant: race, gender, family ties, geography, government, and political boundaries.

In the old covenant, sins were "remembered" every year in the annual Day of Atonement sacrifices (see Lev. 16 and Heb. 10:1–4). In the new covenant, God will "remember their sins no more" (8:12).[53] A soul can now stand before God without condemnation (Rom. 5:1–2), being forgiven of his transgressions through the blood of Christ (Eph. 1:7).

The "new" covenant demands that the "old" covenant be removed or made obsolete (8:13). The writer speaks of it in a gradual sense, however: "growing old" and "ready to disappear [or, near to vanishing away]." In just a few years (AD 66–70), when Judea revolted against Rome and Jerusalem fell to the Roman army, all the functional elements of the Law were destroyed. At that time, God permanently removed the old system. Today, only the "new" covenant (the gospel of Christ) is in force.

Questions

1.) While the Law made (or ordained) men to be high priests, the process involved no specific "oath" (7:20–22). Likewise, Jesus needed no ritual ordination process (see Lev. 8—9) to become High Priest. Why didn't God simply instruct Jesus to be a High Priest in a (new) law as He did for the ancient priests in the Law of Moses?

2.) For what reasons did the "old" covenant need to be superseded by a "new" covenant?

    a. Was the "old" covenant simply terminated (ended) or was it fulfilled? What is the difference and why is this important?

    b. If God only forgives sins through the "new" covenant, what does this say about any different covenant, gospel, plan of salvation, etc. that claims to do the same thing? (Consider John 14:6, Acts 4:12, and Gal. 1:6–8 in your answer.)

3.) What are the "better promises" of the new covenant in comparison to those of the old (8:6)? Does the fact that we have "better promises" than the ancient Israelites mean that God shortchanged them in any way? Please explain.

Lesson Nine:
A New Covenant in Christ's Blood
(9:1–22)

To highlight the supremacy of Christ's priesthood over that of the Levitical system, the *Hebrews* writer now compares the role of the high priest in the Mosaic tabernacle with what Christ has done in the heavens. The Levitical high priest ministered within a physical-based system that merely reflected heavenly designs. The best he could do to intercede for Israel was to enter the throne room of God within that tabernacle—the Holy of Holies. Christ, however, entered the *literal* presence of God and presented Himself *in person* to intercede for all who identify with Him.

The Original Tabernacle as a Type Prophecy (9:1–10): Yet even though the first tabernacle was a physical, man-made structure (see Exod. 25 – 27), it manifested heavenly *realities* through physical *symbols* or *representations* (9:1–5). The "outer" tabernacle refers to the Holy Place, the first room one encountered when entering the sanctuary. This room held three pieces of holy furniture: the golden altar (a.k.a. altar of incense), the seven-lamped candelabra, and the table of showbread.[54] Beyond this was the innermost sanctuary, known as the Most Holy Place or Holy of Holies, in which (in the original tabernacle) was kept only the ark of the covenant.[55] A heavy and richly ornamented veil separated the two rooms.[56]

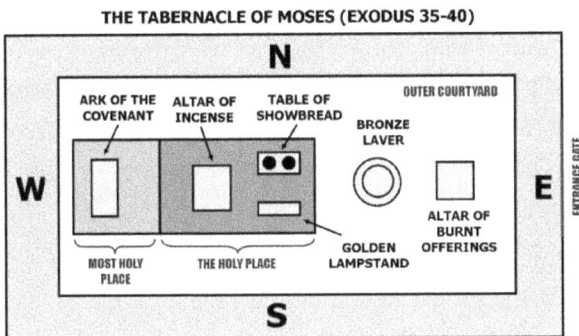

THE TABERNACLE OF MOSES (EXODUS 35-40)

In Moses' day, the ark of the covenant resided in the Holy of Holies and contained a jar of manna (Exod. 16:33), Aaron's almond rod which had budded miraculously (Num. 17:8ff), and the tablets of the covenant (Deut. 10:1–5).[57] By Solomon's day, only the tablets of the Law remained (1 Kings 8:9, 2 Chron. 5:10). By Jesus' day, the ark of the covenant had long since disappeared; no one knows exactly what happened to it (see Jer. 3:16). (The image here is a dramatic re-creation, not necessarily a literal rendition.)

The lid of the ark was called the "mercy seat" which was sprinkled with blood once a year to atone for the sins of the nation of Israel (9:5). In a sense, the ancient high priest was separated from the tablets of the Law (within the ark) by this mercy seat; only blood could serve as the *justifying* or *atoning agent* to reconcile the priest (who represented all of Israel) and God's Law. "But of these things we cannot now speak in detail" (9:5)— for one, because the originals did not exist any longer; for another, because the writer does not want his readers to focus on *signs*, but only uses them to draw attention to *substance*, which is Christ (Col. 2:16–17).

The priests daily used the outer sanctuary of the tabernacle to light the candelabra and burn incense for the daily sacrifice (9:6; see Exod. 30:7–8). Also, every Sabbath the bread on the table of showbread was replaced with twelve fresh loaves (Lev. 24:5–9). But the Holy of Holies was accessed only once a year on the Day of Atonement and *only with blood* (9:7; see Lev. 16). It was here, only on this day and only through the high priest, that the sins of the nation of Israel were removed year by year; otherwise, the tabernacle would be unclean, invalidating all individual offerings for sins on its altar. Without blood—a life offering— the high priest had no permission to enter God's presence and faced divine execution (Lev. 16:2).

The Holy Spirit has revealed these things in Scripture to teach us important lessons (9:8; see Rom. 15:4).[58] The way into the Holy of Holies—in reality, access to the heavenly presence of God—was shrouded in mystery and obscured from human vision, even while the actual tabernacle (temple) remained in Jerusalem. Even so, the physical structure still served as "a symbol for the present time" (9:8)—in other words, it continues to teach lessons.

One such lesson is this: if access to God had been fully realized through the *old* system, there would be no need for a veil or separation within the temple. A better one was needed (and indeed now exists) if that separation was to be removed. Also, the forms and regulations (or gifts and sacrifices) of the old system could cleanse the human conscience; physical rituals cannot overcome spiritual deficiencies (9:9–10). Nonetheless, these things pointed forward to a "time of reformation" or "a new order" or "times of refreshing" (Acts 3:19).

Christ's Presentation in the Spiritual Temple (9:11–14): "But when Christ appeared" (9:11–12)—this indicates a change of status and supersession of the old system. Christ's entrance into the spiritual tabernacle (i.e., the Presence of God) was not accomplished through forms, symbols, or shadows. Instead, He entered this heavenly tabernacle; in so doing, He Himself is the reality and substance of our salvation—the "summing up of all things" (Eph. 1:9–10). His arrival was to present (through the historical event of His sacrificial death) His body and His blood as a sin offering for the whole world (1 John 2:2).[59] In doing so, He secured "eternal redemption" for those who were thus cleansed by His blood (Rom. 5:9, Eph. 1:7, Col. 1:20, etc.).

The critical point is: if the blood or ashes of an animal can (ritually) cleanse the person defiled by sin or death, then the body of Christ can cleanse us absolutely (9:13–14).[60] Animal blood is only a type of what is required for the atonement of human sins; it can only ritually cleanse the human body, but it cannot cleanse the human soul or conscience. Yet Christ's offering does infinitely more than these: His body ("without blemish") and innocent blood cleanse the human conscience of its sin and guilt (or condemnation).[61] Only when we are cleansed by Christ's blood are we able to "serve the living God" with good works (see Eph. 2:10).

Ratification of the New Covenant (9:15–17): "For this reason" (9:15)—since He has accomplished what no man, animal, ceremonial ritual, or earthly sacrifice could accomplish—Christ serves as our new and eternal High Priest. He is both the believer's intercessor *and* sacrifice; His death redeemed all those faithful to the "first" covenant as well as all those who belong to the "new" (or second) covenant.

The word for "covenant" here can also be translated "will" or "testament," such as what one writes before he dies concerning the disposition of his estate.[62] A testament does not have any legal force until the death of the one who makes it (9:16); thus, without that death, the inheritance remains in the hands of the testator (the author of the will).

The analogy here is not perfect, nor was it meant to be, but is only an illustration of what has already been said: just as a testament requires the death of the testator to *bring it to life*, so the new covenant required the death of Christ to *bring it to life*.

"For where a covenant is, there must of necessity be the death of the one who made it" (9:16).
Again, the implication of a *testament* here is for illustrative purposes only; it is not an exact explanation of what has happened. The reasons for this is because:

❑ The covenant is *God's*, not Christ's. Christ offers His blood as the "blood *of* the covenant" (Mat. 26:28, emphasis added) but nowhere is the covenant referred to as His own (see Heb. 12:24 and 13:20).
❑ The Father (the author of the covenant) did not die, but His Son died. The writer consistently identifies God as the Father and Jesus Christ as the Son. God the Father is not *literally* a "testator" (one who makes a last will and testament) but is more accurately a *covenant-maker*.

- ❑ The Son does not offer the covenant, but His blood was necessary to legalize, ratify, or bring the covenant to life. God's covenant of salvation remained only a good idea until Christ died and gave His blood to give *life* to it—and thus, to those *in* it (9:17).
- ❑ Christ did indeed die, but He resurrected from that death. Normally, the testator dies, and his son receives the inheritance. Here it is reversed: the *Son* dies; then something unnatural happens—He rises again. His inheritance (like the believer's) is not in this world but in the heavenly realm.
- ❑ The Father does not disperse all things directly to believers, but has given all things to His Son, who then *shares* His inheritance with those who believe in Him (Eph. 1:13–14).

Blood serves as the most important physical substance on earth because it contains within it the essence of life and God has given it for the very purpose of atonement (Lev. 17:10–11). Therefore, every legal transaction that requires God's justice toward a person's state of condemnation must be satisfied with blood (i.e., life for life).[63]

Even the "first covenant" (God's covenant with Israel) was inaugurated with blood (9:18–20; see Exod. 24:3–8). Upon its dedication, the tabernacle and all its furniture and implements were also sprinkled with blood (9:21; see Lev. 8:15 and 16:14–16). Even the sons of Aaron were cleansed (by both daubing and sprinkling) by blood (Lev. 8:22–24, 30). "Almost" all things in the Law of Moses were cleansed with blood (9:22): a few exceptions involved water or fire as the cleansing agent.[64] But one's induction into a covenant relationship *and* forgiveness of sins (atonement) were never accomplished apart from "shedding of blood."

Questions

1.) If the physical tabernacle constructed by Moses was unable to perfectly overcome the damage of human sin, then what was its purpose?

    a. How did Christ *fulfill* all the symbolism of this tabernacle *and* supersede it?

    b. What did Christ do that no earthly or human priest—or even an angel—could ever do (9:11–12)?

2.) What does it mean to have one's conscience "cleansed" (9:13–14)? According to *what standard*, exactly, is the believer's conscience cleansed—his own or God's?

3.) Throughout Scripture, once *atonement* for sins is made, *service* is expected. One cannot serve the living God, however, with "dead works" (9:14). God allows nothing dead or anything having to do with death in His presence, since this violates His holiness.

    a. Is it possible for a person to serve God who is still "dead" in his sins and has never been cleansed by the blood of Christ (see Eph. 1:7, 2:1–3)?

    b. Can one successfully serve God with a "dead" *faith*—i.e., a mere pronouncement of belief that offers no demonstration or proof of its existence? (Consider James 2:14–26 in your answer.)

Lesson Ten:
Christ's Once-for-all Offering
(9:23—10:18)

Earthly "copies" of heavenly things (i.e., the tabernacle and its furniture and utensils) could not address the full scope of what God required for spiritual atonement (9:23). Even so, these earthly copies needed to be cleansed (or purified) with blood, and animal blood was sufficient for such cleansing.

Yet "better sacrifices" than animal blood and meal offerings were necessary for the redemption of human souls. Christ did not enter the *copy* of heavenly things (i.e., a man-made tabernacle) but heaven itself; His blood does not merely cleanse earthly elements of worship but cleanses the consciences of human souls for worship to God (9:24).

Before offering blood on behalf of the nation of Israel, the ancient high priest first had to offer blood to cover his own sins (9:25). Yet Christ, being sinless, did not have to offer blood for Himself, nor did He have to offer Himself more than once. The writer proposes an absurd situation to make his point: if Christ's once-for-all offering was not sufficient, He would have had to offer Himself many times, from the beginning of time until the end of time (9:26). But this is not necessary since His one offering satisfied all that God required for all time.

Just as men are "appointed...to die" once, so Christ died once (9:27); He does not have to keep dying over and over to sustain what His *once-for-all* sacrificial death accomplished. While a person's death is inevitable, as the result of the curse against his physical *life* (Gen. 3:17–19, Rom. 8:10), Christ's death was self-determined and is life-giving, having overcome the curse (or condemnation) against man's *soul* (Rom. 8:1, Gal. 3:13). He "will appear a second time" (9:28)—what we call His Second Coming (see 1 Thess. 4:13–18, 2 Thess. 1:6–9)—but not to die again. This "second" appearance will be to bring into glory those who "eagerly await" Him (i.e., His faithful followers) *and* judgment to those who refused to obey Him.

Animal Sacrifices Are Inferior to Christ's Sacrifice (10:1–10): "Law" here (10:1) refers to the Levitical sacrificial system of the Law of Moses and its ritual cleansing ordinances. These things were provided for *physical illustrations;* they were *shadows* and *forms*, not the substance (Col. 2:16–17). Animal blood could not redeem the human soul, no matter how many animals or how frequently ("year by year") they were offered. This does not mean that they were not important since God commanded that they be offered, and they did serve a divine purpose. No one who has sinned could (or can) draw near to God without a blood sacrifice to cover his sins.

On the other hand, the fact that blood sacrifices *were* offered repeatedly showed their limitation. These pointed forward to the perfection—a final, all-encompassing, once-for-all sacrifice—of what they could only foreshadow. Until then, they constantly reminded the people of Israel of how far and how often they fell short of God's holiness (10:3). "For it is impossible for the blood of bulls and goats to take away sins" (10:4)—the writer could not have been clearer or more direct in his statement (compare Acts 13:38–39). In sharp contrast, Christ's offering of Himself—and the blood He deliberately shed in doing so—*does* take away sins.

The Body of Christ's Sacrifice (10:5–10): In this passage, the focus is not really on the *act of the consummate offering* itself but the *body (of Christ) that was offered* (Psalm 40:6–8). He could not be an appropriate offering for people without having a *human body.*

We cannot read "sacrifice and offering You have not desired" (10:5) apart from its point of reference. This is a statement of *comparison* or *contrast*, not a renouncing or dismissal of all the ancient sacrifices. God *did* desire sacrifices and offerings—otherwise He never would have commanded them! But God ultimately sought something that mere animal sacrifices and ritual offerings could ever provide: a *perfect sacrifice* through the *willful obedience* of a perfect Man (10:6–7).[65] Things offered by Law (as part of the "first" covenant) could not accomplish this; thus, Jesus came to fulfill the first covenant and establish a better ("second") one in its place (10:8).

The offering of the "body of Jesus Christ" (10:10) refers to nothing less than the literal, factual, historical act of Christ's death upon the cross. He could not have shed His blood if He did not have a body; His body would have been useless if not filled with life-giving blood. This unites Jesus the Son of Man (of earth) with Christ the Son of God (of heaven): His death accomplishes what was needed upon earth as well as in heaven. His death, being complete, perfect, unique, and all-sufficient, serves all people for all time: it is truly "once for all."

Christ's Offering Provides Absolute Forgiveness (10:11–18): The writer continues to contrast the work of the Levitical priest with that of Christ. The emphasis here (10:11) is on the priest who worked *standing up* and Christ who has *sat down*. Every Levitical priest *stood* to minister and offer sacrifices; he never ministered while sitting down. But despite all his standing and ministering, the sacrifices he offered could never "take away sins." Thus, despite his zealous devotion or reverent piety, there was an inherent futility to his work. "Time after time" seems to imply more than mere repetition; it also implies monotony and even exasperation. The prevalence of human sin and defilement forever required his services; he could never sit down (so to speak) because his work was never finished.

But Christ offered His *one sacrifice*, then "sat down at the right hand of God" (10:12; recall comments on 1:3–4). While the priests fearfully entered the Holy of Holies year after year, Christ fearlessly and triumphantly entered its *heavenly reality*—the *true* Holy of Holies, the very Presence of God Himself—and took His rightful seat as both King and High Priest of the kingdom of God. His earthly humility, ministry, bodily offering, and blood sacrifice were once and "for all time" behind Him (2 Cor. 5:16); now He sits on His throne, exercising kingly authority and administering priestly intercession. His work here on earth is done.

There is another part of the great cosmic sequence, however, that has yet to be fulfilled: Christ still waits "until His enemies be made a footstool for His feet" (10:13; see Mat. 22:41–45 and 1 Cor. 15:23–26). God will, in essence, put the necks of all of Christ's enemies "under His feet" (recall comments on 1:13). This is a matter of divine retribution: God cannot allow those who challenge His Son to go unpunished; He must and will defend His holiness through the destruction of those who offend it. This implies a word of warning, too, to the original readers of this epistle: if they make themselves to be enemies of God (through their disregard of His Son's offering), then they also will be the objects of divine wrath.

"For by one offering…for all time" (10:14)—what Christ accomplished was all-sufficient and final. The Holy Spirit, the source of the prophecy quoted from Jer. 31:33–34, has "testified" or confirmed these things to us (10:15–17; recall 8:8–12). Once again, the writer makes a necessary connection between the *blood offering* and *covenant*. God could not have made a covenant with us apart from Christ's blood; yet forgiveness of sins is only obtained through entering a covenant relationship with God. Since those who *are* in covenant with God are forgiven absolutely, there is no need for a further sin offering (10:18).

Questions

1.) To appreciate the magnitude of what Christ *did* in providing Himself as our ideal sacrifice, what are some of the things Christ did *not* do, according to 9:23–28?

2.) If only Christ's bodily offering can atone for human sins (10:10), why do some believers give even greater importance to church activities and good works?

    a. On the other hand, does Christ's atonement render *useless* or *nullify* the need for these other things?

    b. In other words, if redeemed by Christ's blood, are we not *fit* or *qualified* to assemble to worship God and serve in His name?

3.) We know that God *forgives* sins through the "once for all" offering of Christ (10:5–10).

    a. But is anything required of the one who *seeks* this forgiveness? Is forgiveness (and thus, salvation) conditional or unconditional? (Consider Rom. 6:3–7 and 1 John 1:5–10, for example.)

    b. What if one is unwilling to do these things—will God forgive him anyway?

SECTION FOUR:
THE NEED FOR GREATER
FAITH AND ENDURANCE
(10:19 – 12:29)

Lesson Eleven:
Third Warning against Apostasy
(10:19–39)

While the unconverted Jews longed to enter the "holy place" within the literal Jerusalem temple, the Christian has *confidence* to enter something infinitely greater—the holy throne room of God Himself. This is not something he does in person but through what *Christ* did personally.

A New and Living Way to God (10:20–23): "Through the veil" (10:20) alludes to the literal veil (heavy curtain) between the two sanctuaries of the temple. Through that veil the high priest accessed the Holy of Holies. But God has torn that veil in half upon the death of His Son (Mat. 27:51) and has given us access to Him in the Spirit (Eph. 2:18). Instead of attempting to draw near to God through the old system of physical rites and animal sacrifices, we have a "new and living way" by which to fellowship with God (10:20).

Christians do not merely have "a" priest but—to our great advantage—a "great high priest" who serves as a forerunner for us (10:21). He does not minister to a physical temple on earth but presides over "the [heavenly] house of God" and is the head of the spiritual church of God (Eph. 2:19–22). Therefore, instead of drawing *away* from Christ (as the Hebrew Christians were contemplating), the writer gives reasons why believers are to draw near to God *through* Christ (10:22). This should be done "in full assurance of faith" because of what Christ has done as an act of divine grace: He has sprinkled our souls with His blood, purging us of an "evil" conscience (recall 9:13–14; see 1 Peter 1:2).

But to draw near to God also requires the believer's faithful obedience. This requires *at least* that his body be "washed" with pure water, according to the commandment (or word) of God (Eph. 5:25–27, Titus 3:5). While this washing alludes to what was required of the priests in preparation for them to minister to the tabernacle (Exod. 30:18–21), here it has far higher significance. In the context of salvation, "washing" has no legitimate meaning outside of one's baptism into Christ. Elsewhere, Peter explains that this washing/baptism is not for physical cleansing but a spiritual "appeal to God for a good conscience" (1 Peter 3:21).

Our baptism into Christ serves as a "confession" of what we believe about God (who He is, what He has promised, and what He is able to perform) as well as our commitment to Him (who *we* are, what *we* have promised, and our *striving* to perform) (10:23). God acts with divine grace, and we act in human faith: *both* actions are necessary for salvation. Our confession is a binding vow made *to* God (1 Tim. 6:12–13); it is a sacred covenant made *with* God. He is faithful to keep His promises to *us*; the question is, will *we* keep ours to *Him*?

Stimulating One Another (10:24–25): Instead of doubting one's confession and contemplating one's abandonment of Christ, Christians are supposed to discover how to "stimulate" one another to be busy with the business of discipleship (10:24). "Stimulate" in this context means to provoke or prod someone (in a positive way) into doing what is right.[66] Those who focus on "love and good deeds" will get their minds off internal self-doubts, troubles of this life, and even religious persecution. We are to stimulate others *and* be stimulated ourselves to demonstrate love and do good works. To do so is the visible behavior of God's people (Mat. 5:16, John 13:34–35); we are created "in Him" for this very purpose (Eph. 2:10).

"Not forsaking our own assembling together" (10:25).[67] The most natural and contextual understanding of the "day drawing near" phrase is to the weekly assembly. While regularly assembling with sincere believers in public worship does not necessarily prevent one from drifting away, it is almost always true that one who "forsakes [or, abandons; deserts]" this assembling either will or has already begun to "waver." Those who disconnect themselves from the saints (either purposely or out of neglect) sever themselves from the source of teaching, mutual edification, and collective worship that are critical to their spiritual success.

A Most Serious Warning (10:26–31): The writer has thus far used sound reasoning, gentle persuasion, and appeals to the sacred Scripture to convince his readers not to turn away from their commitment to Christ. Now he uses blunt and even terrifying language (10:26–31). He is not describing one who has never been a Christian, or a Christian who continues to *struggle* against sin (as we all do, and not always successfully). Instead, he describes a Christian who *willfully* sins (without repentance) by abandoning altogether his commitment to Christ.

We might understand this passage (10:26) to mean: if a person will not repent of his "willful" sin, then he will face judgment when he dies. Yet, the writer speaks of one's state of existence *even while he lives*: he has no more *opportunity* for a "sacrifice for sins." Sacrifice for sin is not something that benefits a person when he is dead but only while he lives. One who abandons his faith in Christ risks the forfeiture of any further recourse (or atonement) for his sinful state. He has nothing else to look forward to except God's vengeful judgment (10:27). In other words, this passage teaches that a person may reach a point of no return which no penitence can reverse, and for which no prayers can intercede (see 1 John 5:16).

The warning here is grave and intentionally intimidating: *do not incite the wrath of Him who has the power to destroy your soul for irreverence* (see Luke 12:5). "Fire" (10:27) is symbolic of God's judgment against His enemies (which is the context of Isa. 26:11, the quoted citation). To underscore his point, the writer (again) draws upon Israel's own history

(10:28–29). If an Israelite died "without mercy" (i.e., without restraint or pity) for sinning against the Law of Moses[68]—a mere shadow of good things to come—then how much stronger will be the punishment for sinning against the gospel of Christ? (Recall comments on 2:1–4.) This person has forsaken every appeal for divine intercession; he has turned his back on God's finest divine gifts. Through his "willful" sin he (10:29):

- **tramples underfoot the Son of God.** This is not a mere rejection of Christ, but one accompanied with contempt. This willful sinner implies that God is a liar since He endorsed Jesus as His Son (but he now does not believe this—or does not care).
- **regards the "blood of the covenant" as unclean.** He shows no appreciation for Christ's blood to which he once appealed for the forgiveness of his sins.
- **has insulted the Spirit of grace.** To deny the blood of the crucified Christ is to deny the One who has revealed Him through the miracle of revelation and the testimony of miracles themselves.[69]

"For we know Him … " (10:30)—i.e., you Jews already know who God is and what He is capable of.[70] Divine vengeance (a.k.a. retribution, as in 2 Thess. 1:8) is not only something God *will* carry out; because of His absolute moral responsibility to righteousness, He *must* carry it out. He cannot overlook any violation of or insult toward His divine nature or holy character. To "fall into the hands of the living God" (10:31) in the present context refers to an unspeakably dreadful and terrifying experience.

The Need for Endurance (10:32–39): It was necessary for the writer to speak forcefully to the Hebrew Christians. Now, as before (in 6:10), he softens his tone considerably to acknowledge how they had previously shown great faith in times past—the "former days" (10:32). The "great conflict of sufferings" may allude to literal historical persecutions from unconverted Jews and/or the Roman Emperor Nero (reigned AD 54–68). Having received Christian baptism, these Jews were excommunicated from the Jewish community; having pledged allegiance to Christ as Lord, they were charged by Rome with treason against the emperor. Even if they themselves had not faced persecution directly, they had stood by (and identified with) those who had.[71]

Previously, these Christians "joyfully" accepted such hardships, despite the losses (of property, reputation, civil rights, and human dignity) which they incurred (10:34). They looked ahead to what lay beyond this life for their compensation for losses and reward for faithfulness (see Heb. 11:13–16). Nonetheless, even though their lives had been spared (see Heb. 12:4), they had grown *disillusioned* with the source of their confidence through these protracted difficulties. Battle-weariness had set in: while having survived the conflict itself, they are now struggling with the despondency and doubts created *by* the conflict.

The writer (in 10:35–39) makes a tacit allusion to the soldier who, amid the battle, lost his morale, threw aside his shield and sword, turned his back on the enemy, and ran for his life. Such is an act of lost confidence as well as self-preservation. In ancient times, this was considered an extremely shameful act; those who carried it out were often humiliated later and shunned by society, if not outright executed.[72] One's *confidence* in the Rewarder is necessary if he is to receive the great reward for his own efforts—in this case, his unwavering faith (10:35; see Heb. 11:6).[73]

"For you have need of endurance…" (10:36)—a blunt but necessary admonition. The Hebrew Christians had already overcome a number of former trials (perseverance) but they have not yet finished what they started (endurance). They had promised to uphold the "will of God," regardless of the difficulty or cost. One who will not conform to the will of the Father certainly will not receive what He promised (Mat. 7:21–23). The *promise*, then, is conditional; it is contingent upon continued faithfulness.

In time, the writer reminds his readers, "He who is coming will come" (10:37–38). Specifically, this may refer to: a private judgment against these Christians (recall 10:27); Christ's judgment against the nation of Israel (Mat. 24:27–31); or His Second Coming (recall 9:28). Regardless, all three necessitate the same things: faithfulness, preparedness, confidence, endurance, holding fast to one's confession, etc.

The quote here from Hab. 2:3–4 emphasizes God's great displeasure with those who "shrink back" from Him. (Paul used the same quote positively in Rom. 1:17.) Just as God (in Habakkuk's day) would not spare the lives of faithless Israelites who were under attack from the Chaldeans (Babylonians), so He will not save faithless Christians who abandon their confidence in His Son.

"But we are not of those who shrink back…" (10:39)—i.e., the writer gives all benefit of doubt to his readers that they will not succumb to the temptation to forfeit their reward. The abandonment of one's faith is simply not consistent with those who claim to be God's people. Faith is never about shrinking back (or retreating) but always about moving forward (or advancing).

This all-important subject of *faith*, having been introduced again (recall 4:2 and 6:12), will take center stage as the writer takes time to commend those who *have* confidently endured through faith (chapter 11).

Questions

1.) Since Christ has provided for us a "new and living way" to the Father, how should we regard our day-to-day walk with God (see 2 Cor. 4:17)? Should we allow the monotony and tedium of everyday *earthly existence* to bear negatively on our ever-new relationship with the Lord?

2.) Often in our discussions on "worship" we focus only on certain practices: communion, prayer, singing, preaching, and contribution. These are biblical and legitimate functions which support the mission of the church. And yet:

a. Is our *service to one another* a form of worship to Christ? (Consider Mat. 25:34–40, Rom. 12:10–11, and Gal. 5:13–14 in your answer.)

b. Is "[stimulating] one another to love and good deeds" an act of worship to God?

c. Might there be other, similar acts of *service* that are also necessary as our "worship" to Christ? (Consider John 13:34–35 or Phil. 2:1–5.)

3.) According to 10:26–31, the unrepentant Christian runs the risk of losing all access to divine grace and mercy (see 2 Peter 2:20–22). Why is this so? Are there really limitations to God's mercy and patience? Please explain.

4.) Notice the *Hebrews* writer does not say to his readers, "What has happened to you was really unfair," but instead, "You have need of endurance" (10:36). Does this show a great lack of compassion on his part? Why would he say such a thing? Please consider if we should tactfully use this approach in response to the following statements:

- "I know I should talk to people about the Lord, but I just get so frustrated with everyone's indifference and cynicism."
- "I just can't seem to find time to study my Bible like I used to."
- "My children (or grandchildren) occupy so much of my attention that my spiritual life is suffering as a result."
- "I used to be a strong Christian, but now my beliefs are riddled with doubts and unanswered questions. I just don't know what to think anymore."
- "There was a time when I would have laid down my life for my brother or sister in Christ. But now, because I see so many hypocrites in the church, I believe every person just needs to look out for himself and forget about everyone else."
- "I'm retired from work, and I deserve to enjoy the rest of my life doing what I was not able to do in the past. Besides, it's time for the younger generation to take up the torch."

Lesson Twelve:
Faith and Those
Who Have Exemplified It
Part 1
(11:1–22)

Nowhere else in the NT is the subject of faith so clearly expounded upon than in the eleventh chapter of *Hebrews*. While Paul emphasized the *requirement* of faith in the process of justification in *Romans*, the *Hebrews* writer speaks of the continued *implementation* of faith in those who have been justified. While the word has not been used much in this epistle prior to now, "faith"—or the lack of it—is the core issue of those to whom the writer has addressed.

While believers are to "walk by faith, not by sight" (2 Cor. 5:7), the recipients of this letter were "walking" by what they *saw*, not according to the way things really *were*. In their eyes, Christianity had run its course, was failing, or simply was not what they thought it would be. They concluded that Judaism must be superior to Christianity and thus were considering a return to it. In doing so, they would have to abandon their faith in what had been promised to them in Christ.[74] It was necessary, then, to speak of the faith that God required of them, if indeed they were to remain in favor with Him.

Faith is (11:1–2):

- ❏ an "**assurance [or, substance] of things hoped for [or, expected].**" God cannot expect anyone to "hope" in Him if He has not provided this reason. But once He *has* provided it (and He has—see John 20:30–31 and Acts 17:30–31), then every person has a credible, factual, and confident basis for his belief.
- ❏ a "**conviction [or, evidence] of things not seen.**" This speaks to the certainty of what cannot be known by (mere) human

observation. But invisible truths are still truths; even the physical world operates on invisible laws, principles, and forces. To deny God's existence only because He is invisible to us is irrational, especially since He is spiritual in nature (John 1:18, 4:24).[75]

❑ **how we, just like "men of old," gain approval.** For "the righteous" to "live by faith" (Hab. 2:4, Rom. 1:17) requires Someone greater than human authority to provide a standard *of* righteousness. To *have* faith is a human decision; to *define* faith is God's business.

Faith is God's measure of one's trust in Him, even though the believer has not yet *received* what was hoped for or *seen* the One who guarantees it (11:3). The writer here begins with a very general example of this: one who believes that "the word of God" created the world exhibits *faith* in God and His supernatural activity (Gen. 1:1–3, John 1:1–3, 2 Peter 3:5, etc.). The visible was created by the invisible; a supernatural Being created the natural world.

Such conclusions are based on what is not humanly observable or reproducible. The only way one can accept God's explanation of "what happened" is *by faith*: there is no alternative. This does not mean one must exercise *blind* faith, for God has provided sufficient evidence of what He has done and requires men to believe rather than see (Rom. 1:18–20, John 20:29).[76] The "men of old"—i.e., the ancients who lived by faith in God—"gained approval [or, obtained a good testimony]" because of their faith in the Creator of the world.

At this point (11:4ff), the writer provides numerous and specific examples from Scripture of those who have indeed lived "by faith." This is helpful to us because we might not at first consider some of the following actions as demonstrations of *faith* but simply of individual *choices*. But the two things do in fact work together: faith *is* a choice. One must choose to be faithful; it is not something forced upon him.

Abel Lived by Faith (11:4): The first personal example offered is that of Abel, Adam and Eve's second son (Gen. 4:1–5). Abel's attitude demonstrated faith in his compliance to what God expected, while Cain's demonstrated something evil (11:4; see Gen. 4:4 and 1 John 3:11–12).[77] God "testified" or approved of Abel's offering by accepting it; in accepting Abel's sacrifice, God also accepted or approved of Abel himself. Abel's blood "still speaks," that is, it continues to offer an illustration to *us* of what "approved" faith looks like.

Enoch Lived by Faith (11:5): The next example offered is of Enoch, the son of Jared and the father of Methuselah, of the seventh generation of Adam through his son Seth (Gen. 5:18–24). Everyone else in the Gen. 5 genealogy "died," but Enoch did not see death and thus avoided both the curse against Adam (Gen. 3:19) and the curse of the Flood (Gen. 6). There is little that is known of Enoch, except that (it appears) he was a preacher of righteousness amid a human population that was growing increasingly hostile to God (compare Gen. 6:6 and Jude 1:14–15). Because of his faithfulness—which, by implication, must have been significant—God "took" him from the earth without having to experience human death.

Faith Is Essential for Pleasing God (11:6): The writer pauses for a moment to reflect on Enoch's example: it is "impossible" to please God without putting faith in Him (11:6). Such faith requires believing that He exists; obeying His commandments; and trusting in His ability to perform in ways that exceed human ability or comprehension. These things must be carried out in visible *actions*. Because God is greater than us and superior to everything that exists in the world, people *ought* to be seeking Him with an active faith. And those who do seek Him believe that they will be rewarded for their pursuit.

Noah Lived by Faith (11:7): The writer's next example of one who lived "by faith" is Noah (whose name means "rest"), the great-grandson of Enoch (Gen. 5:28–29). Noah had never seen a "flood upon the earth" before *the* Flood, nor had he ever seen a massive ark prior to the one which God commissioned him to build (Gen. 6:5–12). He acted in faith, having an assurance that God would do what He said (both in His judgment against the world *and* His preservation of Noah and his family) *and* a conviction in what he had never seen. He also acted "in reverence," that is, in holy fear of a God powerful enough to condemn in judgment *and* save through providence (Luke 17:26–27, 2 Peter 2:5).

Abraham Lived by Faith (11:8–18): Abraham, one of the greatest heroes of Israel, exhibited unprecedented faith as far as the biblical record is concerned. For this reason, he is referred to as the father of the faithful, having produced many "sons" of faith (Gal. 3:6–9, 29). When God told Abraham to do something, *by faith in God* he did it. The first thing God had Abraham do was to *separate himself* from his father's (Terah's) family so that, in essence, God could be his new Father (Gen. 12:1–9). Thus, Abraham left the city-state of Ur in ancient Babylonia and became a nomadic tent-dweller in a foreign land. In other words, he left a man-made city to find a "city … whose architect and builder is God" (11:10).

Even though his hope in human ability (to produce an heir through Sarah) was dead (i.e., due to the human impossibility of it being realized), Abraham's hope in God was very much alive (see Gen. 17:15–22, 18:1–15, and Rom. 4:16–22).[78] We see a progressive narrowing of ideas and context in this entire passage, from general to specific: a *place*, a *land*, a *city*, a *child* (of promise).

But Abraham never saw the *entire fulfillment* of the promise (of a great nation), since he died before it happened. The writer takes this opportunity to expound on that thought for a moment: *so it is for all of us* (11:13–16). All who walk by faith in God are "strangers and exiles [or, aliens]" on this earth (1 Peter 2:11). The "country" and "city" God has prepared for the faithful lies beyond the scope of human grasp or vision (John 14:2–3, 2 Cor. 4:18, Phil. 3:20–21, and 2 Peter 3:13).

The greatest test of Abraham's faith was his decision to give up Isaac, his son of divine promise, in obedience to God's request (11:17–18; see Gen. 22:1–10). God designated Isaac as the critical link to all that lay in

Abraham's future; without Isaac, there would be no national greatness or future blessings to "all the families of the earth" (Gen. 12:1–3).

Abraham did not know how God was going to rectify the problem that Isaac's death would create, but he believed that God *would* rectify it, even if it meant that He would raise his son from the dead. If God can give life to a dead womb and a dead hope, it seemed reasonable to Abraham to believe that God could give life to a dead person. As it turned out, even the *sparing* of Isaac's life serves as a kind of resurrection parable, since he was (in essence) condemned to death but given a new life instead.

Isaac, Jacob, and Joseph Lived by Faith (11:20–22): While Isaac never had to face the difficult testing his father endured, he still lived in faith, believing in the divine promise that directly involved himself and his sons (Gen. 27). Having transmitted this blessing to his son Jacob—whom he was deceived into believing was his son Esau—Isaac manifested faith that God's providence toward his family would continue even after his death.

Jacob also lived with the belief that he was an active participant in God's divine plan (compare Gen. 28:3–4 and 48:4). He knew that, even after his death, the promise would continue through Joseph's sons, Ephraim and Manasseh, who serve (in this passage) as representatives of all the sons of Israel. (Since Joseph had become a "son" to Pharaoh, Jacob gave to his grandsons Joseph's inheritance.) As for Joseph, he saw the future of his family beyond the borders of Egypt, since he asked that, when they finally did leave, they would take his bones with them (Gen. 50:24–25, Exod. 13:19, and Josh. 24:32).

Questions

1.) Will God justify a person apart from his faith? Can he be justified apart from God's grace? Regarding what is *required for salvation*, which is more important: faith or grace? (Consider Rom. 5:1–2, Eph. 2:8–9, and Titus 3:4–7 in your answer.)

2.) Regarding the origin of the physical world, one either believes it was created (based on evidence) or he does not (11:3); thus, one either has faith in the Creator or he only believes what he sees.

    a. Suppose a person claims to believe in a Creator (and a created world) without citing any evidence for this. What is the problem with this kind of reasoning?

    b. Now suppose a person claims to live by "facts only" and will not believe in anything that requires faith. How does this person's reasoning contradict itself? (In other words, can he truly substantiate everything he knows and believes in with absolute facts?)

3.) Notice the progression (11:7): Noah—being warned—prepared an ark—condemned the world [i.e., by his actions]—became an heir of righteousness. How does this same progressive action apply *in principle* to Christians today?

4.) If Abel, Enoch, Noah, Abraham, and Joseph had not *proved* their faith in God through visible actions, then would God have considered them to be *faithful* to Him? What about *your* faith: does He also require proof of its existence?

Lesson Thirteen:
Faith and Those
Who Have Exemplified It
Part 2
(11:23–40)

Moses Lived by Faith (11:23–28): The next great hero of Scripture after Joseph is unquestionably Moses. Yet, the writer begins this account with the faith of Moses' parents (11:23), Amram and Jochebed (Exod. 6:20). Pharaoh, to keep the Hebrews from revolting against him, ordered that all the male babies be put to death (Exod. 1:16, 22). Amram and Jochebed, however, hid Moses for three months, then put him in a basket in the Nile River, hoping that he would be delivered through some other means.[79]

God *did* preserve Moses through the compassion of Pharaoh's own daughter (Exod. 2:1–10). But when Moses grew up, he exhibited his own personal faith in Jehovah rather than the pagan religion of Egypt. According to Stephen's account (Acts 7:24–29), we know that Moses presupposed some facts about this deliverance, yet after killing an Egyptian he was forced to leave Egypt. Even so, he never abandoned his faith in Jehovah.

Forty years later, God appointed Moses to lead His people out of Egypt accompanied by great demonstrations of His power. Moses was instructed to keep the Passover observance, even though the tenth plague (death of the firstborn of Egypt) was unprecedented and difficult even to imagine (11:28; see Exod. 12). So it was with the parting of the Red Sea: this was unprecedented and impossible by any human effort. But Moses believed the Lord and acted in faith, and Israel walked a dry path through the middle of the waters as a result (11:29; see Exod. 14). Through this one miraculous event, God not only saved Israel but also destroyed the strength of Egypt.

Joshua Lived by Faith (11:30): While the writer does not mention Joshua by name in this next example, he certainly is implied (11:30). It was he before whom the "angel of the LORD" appeared with instructions concerning how to defeat Jericho (Josh. 5:13 – 6:5). Joshua was faithful to keep God's commandment concerning this, even though what he was asked to do was unprecedented and defied any natural explanation. We also cannot ignore the faith of all those who marched *with* Joshua around that city—the Israelite army as well as the priests.

Rahab Acted by Faith (11:31): Rahab, even though a prostitute and a Canaanite—and therefore under a divine curse—played an impressive role in the unfolding plan of God (11:31). Not only is she one of the few women in the OT mentioned for her faith (see Josh. 2 and 6), she also is included in the genealogy of Christ (Mat. 1:5). As Joshua's men spied out the city of Jericho, she believed in God and what He was planning to do and sought redemption for her and her family. For her courage and faith, she is honored here (and in James 2:25).

Others Who Lived by Faith (11:32–38): The next group of examples of faith is not in chronological order, nor is this necessary. The writer may have simply recalled these Bible figures from memory. Some of those mentioned had serious character flaws—think of Samson, for example—and yet they are honored here not because they were flawless, but for the *faith* they exhibited.

- ❑ **Gideon** [a.k.a. Jerub–baal], with only 300 men, overwhelmed a Midianite army that seemed innumerable and invincible (Judg. 6 – 8).
- ❑ **Barak** fought successfully against the Canaanites, trusting in divine counsel through the prophetess Deborah (Judg. 4 – 5). (While Deborah's role goes unmentioned here, it is necessarily implied. The Hebrew readers would certainly know this.)
- ❑ **Samson** repeatedly fought against the Philistines, and especially sought justice against them for gouging out his eyes—a retribution which cost him his own life (Judg. 13 – 16). Even though Samson's reasons for acting were not always virtuous, he believed that God's

power was the source of his own strength.

- ❏ **Jephthah** fought successfully against the Ammonites and punished the arrogance of Ephraim (Judg. 11 – 12). Jephthah did not always appear to be a model of virtuous character, but he did manifest great faith in God—even to his own hurt.
- ❏ **David**, successor to King Saul and the father of Solomon, was the most prominent and one of the most faithful of all the Israelite kings. During his reign he enlarged Israel's borders, defeated all his enemies, and established a kingdom that God has continued even to this day (in Christ; Luke 1:31–33). He was not only Israel's great king, but also served as a spiritual leader and foreshadow of an even greater Messiah.
- ❏ **Samuel and the prophets:** Samuel (1 Sam. 2:18ff) is considered the head of a long line of prophets among Israel (Acts 3:24). Previously, Israel's leaders were often judges; Samuel served as both judge *and* prophet (Acts 13:20). "The prophets" includes not only those whose oracles or books remain today as part of the Hebrew Bible, but also those mentioned within OT history (such as Nathan, Elijah, Elisha, Micaiah, etc.).

Now the writer turns his attention from specific names to specific acts that were *accomplished* through faith (11:33–35a). For example, the faithful:

- ❏ **conquered kingdoms:** think of men like Joshua and David.
- ❏ **performed acts of righteousness [or, administered justice]:** think of the judges, Samuel, David, Solomon, Josiah, and several other righteous kings.
- ❏ **obtained promises:** think of Abraham, Isaac, Jacob, Joseph, Joshua (Josh. 23:14), Hannah, David, and many others.
- ❏ **shut the mouths of lions:** think of Daniel (Dan. 6), but also consider Samson and David, who both single-handedly killed lions (Judg. 14:6, 1 Sam. 17:34–37).
- ❏ **quenched the power [or, fury] of fire:** think of Daniel's friends Shadrach, Meshach, and Abednego (Dan. 3).
- ❏ **escaped the edge of the sword:** think specifically of David

(numerous times), Elijah (from Jezebel; 1 Kings 19:8–10) and Elisha (2 Kings 6:31–32), even though many unrecorded accounts could satisfy this description, including the extra-biblical history of Mattathias and his sons (a.k.a. the Maccabees) in the 2nd century BC.

- **despite personal weakness became strong:** think of Samson, David (despite Bathsheba and other downfalls), and the post-exilic Jews who, despite the humility of captivity, overcame great obstacles and difficulties. We should not forget NT examples as well, especially that of Paul (2 Cor. 12:10) and several of his fellow workers.
- **became mighty in war:** think of Joshua, Caleb, several of the judges, Saul, David, and several more of the kings of Israel and Judah.
- **put foreign armies to flight:** think of Gideon, David (especially regarding the Philistines, after the defeat of Goliath), and several other kings of Israel and Judah.
- **women received back ... resurrection:** think of the women who sheltered Elijah (1 Kings 17:24) and Elisha (2 Kings 4:8–37), whose sons were raised from the dead as a direct result of their faith in God and His prophets.

Having offered examples of great acts of faith, the writer now turns his attention to what men and women have *suffered* because of their faith (11:35b–38). For example, the faithful have endured:

- **torture:** While there are no specific OT examples of this, "torture" can have different meanings than just external, physical affliction (consider Lot, for example, in 2 Peter 2:7–8). The point is: men and women suffered for their faith in various ways, not willing to let go of their faith in God even under great duress or threat of martyrdom. This passage (11:35) alludes to a basic understanding that the loss of one's life here would lead to the gain of a better life in the hereafter— thus, a "better resurrection" than simply prolonging one's typical earthly existence.
- **mockings [or, jeers], scourgings [or, floggings], chains, imprisonment:** think of Jeremiah (Jer. 20:2), Micaiah (1 Kings

22:27), John the Baptist (Mat. 14:3), Jesus, the apostles, Paul, Silas, and no doubt many others. Most of the OT prophets faced ridicule, and sometimes physical abuse, for their roles as God's spokesmen; several of the NT preachers did not fare any better.

- ❏ **stoning:** think of Naboth (1 Kings 21:10–15), Zechariah,[80] Stephen, Paul, and no doubt many others. Stoning was a common method of execution among the Jews (see Mat. 21:35).
- ❏ **being sawn in two:** according to Jewish tradition, the prophet Isaiah was put into a hollow log (or between two boards) which was then sawn in two.[81] Other than this, no other specific incident is known to us, but actual incidents may have been known to the *Hebrews* writer (based upon 2 Sam. 12:31 and 1 Chron. 20:3).
- ❏ **temptation:** think of Joseph (with Potiphar's wife) or Moses (with the treasures of Egypt). Also consider every man and woman who at some time or another has had to decide between the seduction of the world and obedience to God—and chose obedience. More specifically, consider every instance where a servant of God has been faced with death because of his faith, and was tempted to recant his faith in order spare his life (but did not).
- ❏ **death by the sword:**[82] think of the many prophets who were killed in Elijah's day during Jezebel's campaign to eliminate them (1 Kings 19:10). Think also of the priests whom Saul slaughtered (1 Sam. 22:19), Uriah the prophet (Jer. 26:20–23), John the Baptist, Paul (according to tradition), and no doubt many others.
- ❏ **going about in sheepskins, goatskins, etc.:** think of Elijah and John the Baptist, but likely many others also fit this description. The implication here is that of humility, destitution, and severe hardship.
- ❏ **wandering in deserts, mountains, caves, and holes in the ground:** think of David and his men (1 Sam. 24:1), Elijah (1 Kings 19:4), Obadiah and the prophets (1 Kings 18:4, 13), John the Baptist (Mat. 3:1–4), and undoubtedly many others, including Jesus (Luke 9:58).

Approved by Their Faith (11:39–40): In the beginning of this discourse (recall 11:2), the writer declared, "For by it [faith] the men of old gained approval." Even so, such men (and women) did not receive *in this life* the entirety of what was promised them (11:39–40). They believed in God's promise without having seen God, the future, or their own salvation (recall 11:1). They also believed that the promise was worth more than what this world could give them, and that believing in God was far superior to believing in anything or anyone else. In many cases, they put their lives on the line—or even forfeited their lives altogether—based on this belief. The *full* promise, which takes in the big picture perspective, was never realized during their lifetime.

Today, we have far more insight, perspective, and knowledge than these "men of old" ever had because of Christ and the gospel message revealed from heaven. Christ has not only fulfilled the signs and types known to the ancients; He also provides irrefutable support for all that *we also* have been promised (Acts 17:30–31, Eph. 1:13–14). He is our "something better," having provided us a better covenant and better promises (recall 8:6). Thus, the ancients were not "made perfect" *before* or *instead* of us (Christians), but *with* us (recall 9:15). The faithful of any era are "made perfect" through the offering of Christ (Rom. 3:23–25).

Questions

1.) While living in Egypt, Moses believed that Israel's deliverance was near, but he could not make it happen by his own power. Forty years later, God called Moses to lead Israel out of Egypt, but Moses responded with great hesitation. In both cases, Moses maintained his faith in Jehovah but struggled with *how* and *when* God would enact His will.

    a.   Do we still struggle with these same things today? Does this mean we do not really *have* faith in God? Or are there other reasons to account for this?

    b.   Is God required to explain to our satisfaction every detail of how and when He will perform for us to have faith in Him? Why or why not?

2.) God caused the walls of Jericho to fall because the men of Israel believed in God and thus did what He told them to do. But suppose the men had not marched around the city as they were directed—would the walls have collapsed? Or suppose Rahab had not acted on the spies' instructions—would she and her family have been spared? In other words, will God act on behalf of one who refuses to obey what He commanded him or her in the first place? Please explain.

3.) Why does God allow His people to be subjected to hardships and brutality (11:35b–38)? Does this translate to a lack of *concern* or *compassion* on His part? Please explain.

4.) In reading this last section (11:35b–38), we might wonder to ourselves: "How could *I* ever endure such horrific circumstances? Would *I* remain faithful if pushed to those extremes?"

    a.   Should we believe that God will not put us in circumstances that would overwhelm our faith in Him? Is not this itself a part *of* our faith?

    b.   On the other hand: if God does allow us to undergo difficult circumstances for His name's sake, should we trust that God knows that we can endure far more than we ever thought possible? Is not this *also* a part of our faith?

Lesson Fourteen:
The Need for Focus and Discipline
(12:1–17)

Fixing Our Eyes on Jesus (12:1–3): Having provided such powerful examples of faith, the writer now makes a practical application to his readers (12:1). Many "witnesses"[83] continue to speak of their own personal faith and experiences, much like Abel's blood still "speaks" to us (recall 11:4). Collectively, these faithful men and women form a great "cloud" or host which looks down upon the living (so to speak) in anticipation of our own obedience of faith. Or they serve as a figurative crowd of cheering spectators who, having run their own race, now encourage those who have yet to finish theirs.

To "lay aside every encumbrance" (12:1) is an allusion to the Greek Olympics, where the athletes ran in the nude (or nearly so), without any unnecessary clothing impeding their stride. Whatever hinders our discipleship to Christ must be removed (Mat. 5:29–30); we cannot "run" with impediments, distractions, or stumbling blocks getting in the way of our progress. "And the sin … "—not just "sin" in general, but *the* sin ("the" is in the Greek text). This undoubtedly refers to *unbelief*, the specific sin about which the writer has already warned (recall 3:12–13, 19). The entanglement or overwhelming of unbelief will ruin a Christian's effectiveness and will prevent him from reaching his intended goal (2 Tim. 2:4–5, 4:7).

The secret to success is to "[fix] our eyes on Jesus" (12:2; recall 2:10). Thus, the *Hebrews* writer admonishes the Jewish Christians to look beyond their present distractions (and one another) and re-focus intently on Jesus. By implication, he admonishes us to do likewise (1 Tim. 4:10). Jesus Christ is the origin (or author) and completion (or perfecter) of our faith: what we believe (and why we believe it) begins and ends with Him (Rom. 10:4).

Jesus did not look upon the *cross* with joy but found tremendous joy in *obeying His Father.* Whatever that obedience required, even if death on a cross (Phil. 2:7–9), He was willingly compliant: "Your will be done" (Mat. 26:39). "Despising [or, scorning] the shame" probably means: the Jews who crucified Jesus meant to ridicule and humiliate Him, but He was not destroyed by this, as they had hoped.[84] Instead, He turned this situation on its head and made His cross a symbol of great power, glory, and success (1 Cor. 1:18, Col. 2:15). Having been victorious over all His enemies, He "has sat down" to reign as King (recall 1:3) because His earthly work was completed.

"For consider Him who has endured …" (12:3)—in other words, Christ serves as a powerful example to the rest of us. His unspeakably brutal ordeal on the cross was more than compensated by His being exalted by His Father to the highest position in heaven. No one else's trials can compare to His; nonetheless, He promises that every faithful Christian will *share* in His glory, even though they will never have to pay its *cost* (Rev. 3:21). These promises are given "so that [we] may not grow weary and lose heart." To lose one's heart implies feebleness, faintheartedness, and excessive doubt (Gal. 6:9); it is the opposite of faith and courage.

A Father's Discipline of His Sons (12:4–11): While the Hebrew Christians had indeed faced some great trials, and some had suffered loss for the sake of their faith, they had not yet suffered the loss of blood—i.e., their lives had been spared (12:4). Their "striving" was real, but it was not yet over—and (the writer implies) it is not time to *stop* striving.[85] Their struggle was "against sin"—whether sin in general or the specific sin of unbelief that the writer has been addressing throughout the entire epistle.

Christ shed blood in His resistance of the world; many of His followers would likewise resist sin even to the point of death. The Hebrew Christians will not be prepared to follow Christ in faith—even to the point of death (Rev. 2:10)—if they allow themselves to be "encumbered" with doubt and weariness.

These Christians have need of endurance, and one thing that will produce endurance is *discipline* (12:5–6). We often view "discipline" in a negative sense, as in uncomfortable correction or punishment for something wrongly done. While discipline can involve this, it also refers to the structure and stability that supports and strengthens one's belief system. This involves instruction (Col. 2:6–7), diligent application of virtue (2 Peter 1:5–7), and self-mastery (2 Tim. 1:7). Unfortunately, when these habits are missing, or if one has slacked in employing them, corrective or punitive discipline will be necessary.

This is true in the present case: the Hebrew Christians were to be strong and mature, but they had instead become "dull of hearing" (recall 5:11–12). This is unacceptable behavior for "sons" of God—and since they *were* sons, God would *treat* them like sons and discipline them as needed. God does not give His sons what they *deserve*; He gives them (in the form of admonition, correction, or other means) what they *need*. The Scripture citation is from Prov. 3:11–12; Christ later cites from this same passage (Rev. 3:19).

A father who does not discipline his son is not showing genuine *love* (12:7), since "sonship and fatherly chastisement invariably go together."[86] If God did not discipline His own sons, then it would indicate that this alleged "sonship" is in fact illegitimate: sons who are not disciplined are really not sons at all (12:8).[87] If one's sonship is questioned, then so is his inheritance (Gal. 4:7).

A Christian should not assume that *any* adversity he faces is automatically godly "discipline." Sometimes it is our own guilty conscience that reads "divine chastisement" into a particular hardship we may be facing. Far more often, we face adversity simply because we live in a sinful world *and* because we stand opposed to that world in our faith. And, sadly, what we think is God's discipline may be the consequences we face from our own foolish choices.

On the other hand, it appears that God is getting the Hebrew Christians' attention with very real (but undisclosed) discipline to send a strong message: *you are going in the wrong direction.* Earthly fathers discipline their sons for (ideally) good reason: to direct them away from destructive behavior and redirect them toward proper behavior. Since this is acceptable of earthly fathers, it is especially so of our heavenly Father, whose knowledge of what is "good" is far superior to that of any earthly father (12:9–10; see Mat. 7:9–11).

Earthly fathers, for all the good that they do, cannot save their children's souls; our heavenly Father has both the *ability* and *desire* to save our souls (1 Tim. 2:4). Earthly fathers prepare their children for this life, but our heavenly Father prepares us for the life to come, so that in all things "we may share His holiness." Thus, there is a direct connection between *preparedness* and *drawing near to God in holiness* (see 2 Cor. 5:5 and 1 Peter 1:13–16).

Of course, no one *likes* corrective discipline (12:11). It is often painful and sorrowful. Yet the outcome, when properly administered and properly received, is the refinement of our souls (James 1:2–4). Furthermore, all such discipline is limited to this life on this earth; it is temporary and finite; it will not be necessary in the life to come. Discipline produces pain, sorrow, and loss; but the ideal *result* of discipline is "the peaceful fruit of righteousness." Just as fruit takes time to mature and ripen, so the "fruit of righteousness" will not develop immediately. Yet, over time, it will be for the believer exactly what he was looking for all along.

Desired Response to God's Discipline (12:12–17): God does His part—i.e., whatever discipline is needed to redirect the soul—but the Christian must also do *his* part (12:12).[88] The writer makes another strong admonition to the recipients of his epistle: they had not finished the race, yet they were already tired and weary; they ought to be strong, but instead they were weak and appeared untrained (recall 5:11–12). This deterioration (atrophy) of their spiritual lives threatened their inheritance with God. Weak, under-prepared, and spiritually lame Christians will not finish their race. God's grace is the source of spiritual strength, healing, and forgiveness, but God does not do for a person what he is able (and instructed) to do for himself (12:13).

"Pursue peace with all men" (12:14)—literally, follow it, as though it were leading (you) in a certain direction. Spiritual peace is only obtainable through a right relationship with God (Rom. 5:1–2), and this relationship requires our most serious time, effort, and commitment. But the writer here speaks to the peace we are to pursue "with all men"—i.e., the peace we have *within*, because of our right relationship with God, must be extended to others. Initially, we are to seek peace with fellow believers (Rom. 14:19); secondarily, to "all men" (see Gal. 6:9–10). Peace, rather than strife, contention, and enmity, is the noble characteristic of all genuine sons of God (Mat. 5:9).

To be at peace *with* God requires that one be sanctified *by* Him. It is impossible to pursue peace without first seeking sanctification (the process of being sanctified or made holy). While we have a part to play in achieving holiness (see 2 Cor. 7:1 and 1 Peter 1:13–16, for example), it is God who *makes* us holy. No one can be sanctified (made holy) apart from the work of divine grace. Since no one who is unholy will "see the Lord" (i.e., favorably stand in His presence), those who are God's people must also be holy. Sanctification implies purity, and purity is necessary to walk in fellowship with the Lord.

To "come short of the grace of God" (12:15) means to forfeit God's divine favor by failing to appreciate or implement it. A Christian can "come short" of saving grace through impenitence, negligence, self-righteousness, arrogance, or simply an excessive preoccupation with lesser things. He is supposed to be strengthened by grace and grow in it (2 Tim. 2:1, 2 Peter 3:18); if he is not being strengthened, he is weakening; if he is not growing, he is dying.

Disqualification is a real possibility, even for those who have preached God's word to others (1 Cor. 9:27, in principle). A "root of bitterness" refers to the foothold that sin makes in a person's heart: it begins as a root, searching for a firm attachment, but then grows into an insidious and noxious weed when it "springs up."[89] Yet God's grace, when one fully embraces it, makes him invincible to falling away from the truth (or "stumbling," as in 2 Peter 1:10–11).

Scripture does not have any approving things to say about Esau (12:16–17). Esau represents the secular, earth-bound, worldly mentality that stands in opposition to God, just as the Edomites (descendants of Esau) several times stood opposed to Israel (Exod. 17:8–16, Num. 20:14–21, etc.). The writer does not mean that Esau himself was sexually immoral (although this might be a reference to his marriage choices; see Gen. 26:34–35). Yet fornicators and unholy people fall into the same category: they both have a disregard for what is proper and sacred.[90] Esau demonstrated this disregard when he sold his divine birthright for a single meal. What he forfeited, he never recovered, even though later he bitterly regretted it (see Gen. 27:30–40).[91]

In a similar vein, the Hebrew Christians were attempting to forfeit their inheritance with God for an inferior and obsolete religion (Judaism)—a bowl of stew in comparison to the promises of inheritance with Christ.

Questions

1.) What does the depiction of the Christian life as a "race" imply (12:1)? (Consider a literal footrace, and then make the spiritual applications.)

2.) What causes Christians to "grow weary and lose heart" (12:3)? What happens (ultimately) to those who do "lose heart"? How are we instructed to *overcome* such weariness and faintheartedness?

3.) God will punish sinners, but He disciplines His "sons" (12:5–11). What is the difference between the two actions?

4.) "Peace" and "sanctification" are *essential* for anyone who wishes to "see the Lord" (12:14). But what do peace and sanctification look like in a Christian's life? Who *decides* what these should look like?

5.) We are not to "give the devil an opportunity" to take advantage of us (Eph. 4:27). Do deliberate weakness, laziness, negligence, doubt, and bitterness provide golden opportunities for him to do this (12:15–17)? Please explain.

Lesson Fifteen:
The Unshakable Kingdom
(12:18–29)

The Physical Mt Sinai (**12:18–21**): Having made strong statements, the writer now relaxes his approach and moves toward positive things. The purpose of his instruction is to help prepare his readers for their presentation before God (12:18–21). He likens this to the occasion of Israel's presentation before God at Mt Sinai (Exod. 19 – 24). On that occasion, God needed to contrast His holy nature against that of worldly Israel—and He did so with a frightening display of fire, smoke, thunder, and lightning. Three major points here:

❑ Israel had to *prepare* themselves to be in God's presence (Exod. 19:10–11, 15). They could not simply "show up" in their casual clothes, so to speak (like so many people do today for church services), but they had to be washed, separated from sexual activity with their spouses, and "be ready" to meet the Lord. God was not coming to meet *them*, but *they* were coming to Sinai to meet *Him*.

❑ The Israelites could not come any closer to God than He allowed. Boundaries were set up at the base of Mt Sinai to prevent any person (or even an animal) from touching the mountain, which was designated a holy place because of God's presence there (Exod. 19:12–13).

❑ God spoke His ten commandments to the people with His own voice (Exod. 20:1, 22). This thundering sound—accompanied with the smoke, lightning, and actual thunder—proved to be too much for the people. They begged Moses to speak with God himself rather than them having to endure this any further (Exod. 20:18–22; see Deut. 5:4–5).

God's holy presence demanded the Israelites' utmost reverence and respect; He threatened them with *death* if they failed to obey Him. Thus, a careless or unbelieving person—i.e., one with a disposition like Esau's—would have been destroyed. Even though God now speaks to us "in His Son" (recall 1:2), it is still *God speaking*. While Jesus' demeanor seems far less threatening than what the Israelites encountered at Sinai, we are not to think that His authority or power has diminished.

The Spiritual Mt Zion (12:22–24): "But you have come to Mount Zion … " (12:22)—i.e., not a physical mountain but a spiritual one, which is the foundation for the holy *city of believers*. "Zion" is the ancient name of one of the hills of Jerusalem; in prophetic context, however, it symbolized the future gathering place of God's glorified people on earth (Isa. 2:2–4). No longer is the literal city of Jerusalem relevant (see John 4:21–24); Christ has built a new "temple-city"—His church—in which all the redeemed who live on earth will dwell (Rev. 14:1–3).

To clarify: "Zion" represents Christ's divine authority; it is the "rock" upon which He will build His church (Mat. 16:18). "Jerusalem" represents the church itself which He has founded upon this "rock"/ mountain. It is a symbolic portrayal of the *physical* church—the assembly of the global brotherhood of Christ on earth—and not (yet) the *heavenly* church which will enter eternal glory after the world has run its course (as in Rev. 21:1ff).

In contrast to the severe, primitive, and earthly context of physical Mt Sinai, Christians have come to a "mountain" of glory, majesty, and thrilling anticipation (12:22–24):

- ❑ It is the **"city of the living God":** This does not merely designate a meeting place but an organized, established, and spiritual community (recall 11:10). This depicts the holy gathering of God's people on the earth—one people, one city, and one King and High Priest, all on one "mountain."
- ❑ It is **"the heavenly Jerusalem":** This is not the literal city of Jerusalem, but one based on its (OT) significance and symbolism. Just as God chose Jerusalem as the place where His people would worship Him (1 Kings 11:13), so the "heavenly" Jerusalem—Christ's physical church on earth—is where God's people will worship Him.

- ❏ Christians have come to:
  - ▪ a spiritual community which is surrounded by angels (recall 1:14).
  - ▪ a great city of God in which His people assemble whose names are enrolled in heaven (Rev. 3:5).
  - ▪ "God, the Judge of all"—He who exonerates those redeemed by Christ's blood but destroys those who refuse this.
  - ▪ a great company of people "made perfect" through God's grace and their obedient faith.
  - ▪ "Jesus, the mediator of a new covenant"—the very One whose blood has brought to life the covenant by which we have fellowship with God.
  - ▪ Jesus' blood, "speaks better than … Abel" (recall 11:4). Abel's blood spoke well of himself; Jesus' blood "speaks" for *us* by atoning for our sins.

Those who are "in Christ" join with this great throng of the redeemed by faith and in promise. It is *real,* but it remains (for Christians in this life) conditioned upon our completion of the "race that is set before us" (recall 12:1). The writer thus implores his readers to consider very seriously what he is saying: *Zion—not Sinai—is the "mountain" to which you were called in Christ!* It is vastly superior to what was defined in the first covenant in every respect.

The Need for Reverence and Awe (12:25–29): The writer reiterates a point made earlier (recall 2:1–3). Moses warned from the earth, threatening physical execution; how much more threatening, then, are God's warnings from heaven, threatening the execution (so to speak) of one's soul![92] To "refuse" God means to stubbornly disbelieve His power and His promises, even though He has provided sufficient reason to believe in them (recall 3:12–19). It is impossible to refuse God's salvation through His Son and be pleasing to Him all at once.

As God's voice shook Mt Sinai, so He will once again shake all Creation (12:26–27), indicating the *removal* of such things (i.e., the end of the physical system). To "shake" here (quoting from Haggai 2:6–7) implies not only God's sovereignty over whatever is shaken but also the temporariness or destructibility of such things. The Creator is eternal and indestructible—He cannot be "shaken" by anyone or anything—but He has the authority and ability to "shake" (or remove) all that has been created (2 Peter 3:7–12).[93]

"Therefore … let us show gratitude" (12:28)—not fear, doubt, unbelief, or indifference. Ingratitude and irreverence always go together: one leads to the other. In other words, instead of critiquing God's heavenly plans through finite, earthly perspectives, Christians are to *give thanks* that He has invited us into His eternal and majestic dwelling place (John 14:1–3). "Acceptable service [or, worship]" is reminiscent of Rom. 12:1–2: both passages refer to the priestly action of offering sacrifices of faith, humility, devotion, and good works to God.

Such holy and priestly service must be with "reverence" and "awe"—i.e., with *devout respect* and with a *healthy fear of God* (Prov. 1:7, Eccles. 12:13, etc.). While some Hebrew Christians thought they could serve God adequately through the Law of Moses, forsaking the holy assembly on Mt Zion displayed *unbelief, irreverence,* and *ingratitude,* not "acceptable service." The same God who consumed unbelievers with fire long ago (Lev. 10:1–3 and Num. 16:31–35) will also—in due time—destroy those who are ungrateful and irreverent to Him in His church (12:29). Solemnity, sacredness, reverence, and preparedness are the biblical hallmarks of the assemblies of God's people.

Questions

1.) What did God impress upon Israel by manifesting Himself before them in the way that He did (in Exod. 19)? Why was this necessary, especially initially? Why has He softened His manifestation to us in Christ?

2.) Today, mainstream "Christianity" emphasizes convenience, comfort, casualness, and the catering to members' preferences. Instead of preparing themselves to come before God because of who *He* is, the attitude is that God needs to accommodate people because of where *they* are.

    a.   Given both Exod. 19 and Heb. 12:22–24, how does this "mainstream" mentality contradict what God expects of His people?

    b.   Are we to think that God has *reduced* expectations for Christians today when in fact we have a far *superior* understanding of His will than what the Israelites ever had? (Consider Luke 12:47–48: with privilege comes responsibility.)

3.) Created things can be destroyed, but the Creator Himself is indestructible. How is this concept plainly understood in 12:25–29? What bearing does this have on those who are redeemed by Christ—will we be preserved or destroyed (1 John 2:17)?

4.) Should "reverence" and "awe" (12:28) characterize Christians' worship assemblies? If not, why not? If so, who determines what "reverence" and "awe" look like and how we are to practice them within the group?

SECTION FIVE:
FINAL ADMONITIONS
(13:1–25)

Lesson Sixteen:
Christian Responsibilities
(13:1–19)

Nearing the end of his epistle, the *Hebrews* writer makes some final admonitions to his readers. His focus is twofold: moral *purity* (to Christ) and moral *responsibility* (to Christians). "Let love of the brethren continue" (13:1)—lit., "keep on loving each other as brothers [in Christ]." There is a critical link between one's devotion to Christ and his love for God's people. "Anyone of the readers who would be inclined to give up Christ and to revert to Judaism would promptly show that decline in faith by coldness and indifference to his Christian brethren."[94] Brotherly love is one of the defining traits of Christians; it is impossible to represent Christ rightly without demonstrating this.

A specific manifestation of Christian love and kindness is *hospitality* (13:2). The Greek word for "hospitality" means "kind to guests" or "lover of strangers." "Strangers" in this context specifically refers to *brethren* who are (previously) unknown to us, such as travelers or missionaries (as in 3 John 1:5–8). The traveling Christians of the first century faced difficulties that we may have trouble appreciating. Inns were of poor quality, ill-repute, or simply scarce in number; thieves laid in wait on the highways; travelers faced wild animals and inclement weather; people lost their lives just "traveling." Thus, the expressed need for hospitality is greater (here) than we might first realize.

The reference to "angels" (13:2) undoubtedly alludes to Abraham and Lot's kindness toward angelic messengers in Gen. 18—19. Many Christians have taught from this passage, however, that "strangers" *we* meet are sometimes angels in disguise, roaming the earth and intersecting with our lives. The context simply does not support this. On the other hand, it *may* be true that God does allow anonymous saints (and even those who are not saints) to cross our paths to give us opportunity to show kindness and hospitality. And it is *always* true that whatever we do for Christ's brethren, we do for Him also (Mat. 25:40).

"Prisoners," likewise, are not common criminals, as people tend to interpret this (13:3). This passage is allegedly the basis for modern "prison ministries" carried out by Christians and churches. While sharing the gospel with guilty criminals is noble, this passage refers to people jailed for their *faith*, not their crimes.[95] One who takes care of such prisoners ought to do so with sympathy and compassion, as though he himself were imprisoned (as might be the case someday). "In the body" seems to refer to the physical flesh, not the body of Christ. In remembering "strangers" and "prisoners," the writer is saying, "Show godly love to fellow Christian travelers, whether or not you had previously met them; reach out to Christians who need your care and are unable to provide for their own needs."

Christians are to practice especially in the privacy of their homes and the intimacy of their marriages (13:4). Marriage is a divinely created institution and a holy union (Mat. 19:6). In effect, it is also both a legal and accommodating provision for the sexual needs of a man and a woman (1 Cor. 7:1–2). "Bed" here is a euphemism for the sexual activity between a husband and his wife.

"Fornicators" and "adulterers" are mentioned separately here since they are not identical (see 1 Cor. 6:9). All adulterers are fornicators, but not all fornicators are adulterers. Fornication is any sexually immoral or deviant behavior, regardless (or even in the absence) of a pre-existing relationship. Adultery specifically involves one who is already in a covenant (marriage) relationship; it is the corruption *of* that covenant through some form of treachery (Mal. 2:14–16) that involves a third party—someone outside of his or her marriage. "God will judge" those who practice such things, since this contradicts the purity of the church (1 Thess. 4:3–8).

Christian love is an excellent virtue and required of God's people. "Love of money" (13:5a) is an unholy love that, if practiced, leads to the ruin of God's people. This "love" seeks contentment in something other than God. Money represents human authority or man-made institutions; the love of money implies a greater trust or confidence in human power than in God's (Luke 12:15, 16:14–15). Not only this, but no one can love both money and God equally; one loyalty will always be greater than the other (Mat. 6:24).

In contrast, Christians are to learn to be content with their circumstances. This does not mean that we can never seek to improve our situation (see 1 Cor. 7:21, in principle) or obtain a higher paying job. Earning money or having money is not the same thing as an unholy *love* for money: one is a responsibility or stewardship, the other is a corruption of the heart. Contentment, in this context, means finding satisfaction in *God* rather than in anything (or anyone) in this world (1 Tim. 6:6, Phil. 4:11–12, etc.). Human pride seeks satisfaction in something other than God; all sin is the result of dissatisfaction with God's provisions. "The love of money is just as much an evil desire as the sexual lust that can violate marriage."[96]

While Christians may disappoint the Lord, He will *never* disappoint us or *fail* to save us (13:5b–6).[97] Such encouragements apply generally and timelessly to God's people everywhere. The connection to the previous admonitions may be this: spouses can fail, and money *will* fail, but God will never fail. While *internal lusts* and *illicit desires* can corrupt our heart (James 1:13–16), no *external threat* can corrupt our salvation (Luke 12:4–7, Rom. 8:35–39).

Those Who Refuse Christ's Supremacy (13:7–14): Instead of returning to Jerusalem and its religion, the Hebrew Christians are to abandon that pursuit altogether. The reason for this would soon be abundantly and historically clear (when divine judgment descended upon the nation of Israel in AD 70). Thus, the writer admonishes them to "remember those who led you" to Christ (13:7), rather than those who lead away from Him, or their sentimental attachment to Judaism. These Christian leaders likely includes church elders, since they are mentioned twice more in this same chapter (13:17, 24); yet in this context it may also include teachers and missionaries of the gospel. In essence, it includes whoever "[speaks] the word of God" to others as a means of converting them to disciples of Christ.

While earthly leaders—like all men—appear for a little while and then fade away, there is one Leader who does not: Jesus Christ (13:8). He is "the same" throughout all time; He is the true and universal *constant* in whom there is no variation, failure, or disappointment. Since He does not change, neither does His gospel. Christ's sacrifice has left nothing undone and satisfies God's requirement for our atonement completely.

The final, most explicit warning (13:9) is connected to the above fact: *since* Christ does not change or disappoint, there is absolutely no reason to turn away from Him. Those who are "carried away" by lesser things have not fixed their eyes on the Author and Perfecter of faith (recall 12:2), the Apostle and High Priest of our confession (recall 3:1). "Varied and strange teachings [or, doctrines]" may refer to the many formalities and traditions of Judaism which were added to the Law as though equal to it (see Mat. 15:3–9). This may have specific reference to dietary restrictions (because of 13:10), but it may also refer to any teachings that are foreign (or "strange") to the gospel of Christ.

Regardless, food and rituals have never *by themselves* been a measurement of fellowship with God (Rom. 14:17). Such external things do not create righteousness or substitute for moral purity (Col. 2:20–23). "Those who were so occupied" refers to the ancient priests who officiated over thousands of sacrifices on the altar. Those sacrifices, necessary as they were at the time, were never the source of spiritual renewal or inward change. God's grace, however, *does* transform the believer's heart to bring about a genuine inward transformation.

"We have an altar from which those…have no right to eat" (13:10). The Levitical priesthood has been superseded (and thus made obsolete) by Christ's high priesthood (recall 8:13). Thus, to continue to partake of that obsolete system and its offerings is offensive to Christ and to the Father whose divine oath has established His new priesthood (recall

7:28). The Christian's "altar" is *Christ on His cross*—a stumbling block to unbelieving Jews and foolishness to the worldly wise (1 Cor. 1:23). Our sacrifice is a *Person*, not an animal; we partake of *His* flesh and drink *His* blood in our remembrance of Him (John 6:53–58, Luke 22:19–20).[98]

Hebrew Christians have *no purpose* to partake of the Levitical offerings; yet those who refuse Christ—in the context, those who cling to the old system—have *no right* to partake of this superior offering.[99] These two systems are incompatible; only one of them is approved by God.

The sacrifice to which the writer specifically refers is a *sin offering* (13:11–12). The ashes of a sin offering were taken "outside the camp" (see Lev. 4:11–12, 16:27). This is because sin is a contaminant and defilement; whatever animal was used in the atonement process was polluted by the sin that it "covered," so that it (the animal's body) had to be fully destroyed by burning. This proves that the animal's body (and, by implication, its blood) was insufficient to *remove* sin (10:4) since its body became corrupted (cursed) like the sins it bore.

Christ's sacrifice follows the same pattern as the sin offerings but succeeds where those offerings never could. His body was offered as the *once for all* sin offering and taken "outside the gate" (of Jerusalem) to die (Luke 13:33, John 19:20). Yet because He was a divine Person, He was able to offer a *perfect* sacrifice, being able to absorb the *penalty* for sin completely in Himself. While He "became [or, represented] a curse for us" (Gal. 3:13), He Himself was not accursed.[100] His body did not become corrupted in the process of atoning for our sins. This is why His flesh did not decay (Acts 2:29–33) and is also why we symbolically eat His body and drink His blood through the partaking of the Lord's Supper (1 Cor. 11:23–26). We could not eat the "flesh" or drink the "blood" of a dead, rotting corpse; in partaking of a *living Savior*, we eat and drink of Him who imparts *life* to us.

"So, let us go out to Him … " (13:13)—i.e., the Hebrew Christians, rather than return to the Law of Moses, must separate themselves from those who practice it in defiance of Christ. By supporting the priestly sacrifices offered within Jerusalem, these Christians identified with those who were under a curse (Luke 19:41–44, 21:20–24). (The curse was upon Jerusalem specifically, but included the entire Jewish nation—i.e., all those unbelieving Jews who rejected Jesus as their Messiah.) Just as men treated Jesus as an outcast and took Him "outside the gate," so the Christian must bear his own mistreatment by unbelievers and take his place alongside Him.

As with the Hebrew Christians, so it is with us: whatever shame or hardship is necessary in identifying with Christ, we must accept this as part of our discipleship to Him. Christ's "reproach" refers to His having been crucified as a blasphemer and a criminal; the Christian also endures a type of crucifixion in his discipleship (Gal. 2:20). We, like the faithful who have gone before us, must not be seeking an earthly city for a permanent home but one "which is to come," one which is not even of this world (recall 11:13–16).

What Is Expected of Believers (13:15–19): While Christ has offered up a sacrifice for our sins, Christians are to offer up a "sacrifice of praise to God" (13:15). Our sacrifices are necessary to render an "acceptable service" of worship (recall 12:28). The "fruit of lips" can mean any spoken praise or thanksgiving as well as prayers (Phil. 4:4–6), songs (Eph. 5:19, Col. 3:16–17), confessions of faith (Mat. 10:32), and all "spiritual sacrifices [which are] acceptable to God through Jesus Christ" (1 Peter 2:5). Spoken praise is necessary, but the ultimate praise to Christ is demonstrated through "doing good and sharing," and especially with those who belong to Him (13:16; compare Gal. 6:9–10).

"Obey … and submit" (13:17)—i.e., accept the counsel of your spiritual leaders and voluntarily put yourselves under their oversight. Given the context, "leaders" here refers to church elders; no other men "watch over your souls" or "give an account" in this manner. The word "rule" means "those who have rule over you"; here it indicates *managerial oversight* and not superiority in rank, worth, or human nature.[101] To "watch" over someone's soul cannot mean to lord oneself over that person, or to impose upon him in any inappropriate or unchristian way (1 Peter 5:2–3).

Often, this passage (13:17) is interpreted to read: "Obey the authority of the elders." While elders are authorized to *oversee* a group, this does not translate to having *authority* over the group—to act with independent and binding authority. Nowhere in the NT does it say that elders are to exercise their *own* authority. They are to shepherd their "flock," but they do not own the flock; they are to serve as managers, not reign as dictators; they are to nurture souls, not act like a police force. Congregations are to "submit" to their elders by *allowing themselves* to be governed by these men whom they have appointed for this very purpose.[102] Likewise, elders are to submit themselves in humility to the needs of the congregation (Eph. 5:21, Phil. 2:1–5). Elders are not kings or despots; they are not above fair criticism or questioning.[103]

Elders *do* have a responsibility to "watch over" the souls of their congregation (13:17). This does not mean they are *responsible* for these souls, as though they were to answer in place of each person, but that they are entrusted with *governing* or *managing* them. "Let them … with joy and not with grief"—i.e., do not make their job unnecessarily difficult by snubbing their concern, rejecting their counsel, or resisting their oversight. This is "unprofitable," since the elders will have to resort to discipline rather than edification. Also, the one causing such trouble will answer to Christ for his interference with the system which He has put into place. Those who were regularly forsaking the assembly of the saints (recall 10:25) are probably among those in need of this admonition.

"Pray for us" (13:18–19)—this indicates that the writer has not lost his confidence in those to whom he is writing, since he would not ask unbelievers to pray for anyone. After providing so much instruction to others, he still recognizes his own need for help. We do not know the writer's personal circumstances, but we do know that he takes his spiritual responsibilities very seriously, and thus puts high emphasis on his own moral conduct. He is not approved by "good conscience" alone; rather, he believes his conscience is "good" only because he has been approved by God because of his faith (recall 11:2; see 1 Cor. 4:3–4).

Questions

1.) Please read Mat. 25:31–46 in conjunction with Heb. 13:1–3. How important to Christ are expressions of love and gestures of hospitality toward His brethren? What impact do these things have in our final accounting to God? What impact does the *lack* of these things have?

2.) Since our society is no longer practicing cultic paganism and temple prostitution (at least, in the same way these happened in the ancient world), are fornication and adultery even relevant issues to discuss among Christians (13:4)?

    a.   Regardless, are all marriages between Christians automatically "held in honor"? Or does "honor" require more than mere marital status?

    b.   Does fantasizing over photographs of nude men and/or women on the internet (for example) constitute as defilement of the "marriage bed"? Please explain.

3.) "'It is good for the heart to be strengthened by grace, not by foods" (13:9). What does this mean, particularly to those to whom *Hebrews* was written? How does it apply to us today, without any specific reference to food? (See Rom. 14:16–17, Col. 2:8, 20–23, and 2 Peter 3:18.)

4.) If elders are to keep watch over the souls of believers, is it necessary that they know those for whom they are responsible (13:17)? If not, then how can they be responsible for a random assemblage of people? If so, then how is this to be done?

5.) How are the two roles—that of elders shepherding a congregation and that of a congregation submitting to its elders—balanced? In other words, how does 13:7 and 13:17 highlight the responsibility of both parties in a healthy, functional, and productive relationship? What can ruin that relationship?

Benediction and Final Thoughts
(13:20–25)

T he writer of *Hebrews* concludes his profound epistle with a magnificent hymn of praise, one that is filled with excellent truths (13:20-21). Having just spoken about the responsibility of church shepherds (elders), he now speaks of the "great Shepherd" who not only watches *over* our souls but *sanctifies* them (1 Peter 2:25, 5:4). This Shepherd has no equal; His power, as displayed in His resurrection, is unprecedented and unparalleled; His blood does what no other blood can do. The "eternal covenant" refers to the salvation God has always provided for those who have called upon Him in faith, from one end of humanity to the other. Every covenant God has made with people finds its fulfillment (or closure) in Christ. The eternal covenant defines the "eternal purpose" in which we have "confident access" to God through "faith in Him" (Eph. 3:11-12).

God never gives us work to do in His name without the heavenly provisions to do it. "Equip" here means to make complete or perfect, or to restore to an ideal state. God performs in *us* so that we can perform for *Him*. Indeed, we have been created anew in Christ for the purpose of performing good deeds (Eph. 2:10). All this is done "through Jesus Christ": He is Lord, we are servants; He is the head of His church, we are mere members of it; He is the Shepherd and Guardian of our souls, and He needs no advice or counsel from us.

The "word of exhortation" (13:22) indicates an appeal to God's word as a means of instruction and edification. If *Hebrews* is a "brief" letter, we can only imagine what the writer would have covered if given more opportunity. "Timothy" may likely be Paul's protégé and was probably well-known throughout the brotherhood at this point (13:23). Regardless, it appears that Timothy may have been in prison and had recently been released. There is no record of this in Paul's letters, since this imprisonment likely occurred after Paul's death (and the *Hebrews* letter was also likely written after his death).

"Leaders" here (as in 13:17) most naturally refers to elders. If the reference is to many elders, it would underscore the likelihood that this letter was sent to a circle of (Christian) *friends* and not to a single congregation. "Saints" are those who have been sanctified by Christ's blood and thus have been added to Christ's body (1 Cor. 2).

The expression "those from Italy" is difficult to interpret with certainty. Does he mean *he* is in Italy, or that he is sending greetings from *friends* who are in Italy? If he himself is in Italy, is he just passing through, or is that where he lives? Thankfully, this matter does not have to be resolved for us to accept the genuineness of this epistle. "Grace be with you all"—a common benediction, implying *we will overcome only with God's divine help.* Divine grace does everything for us that we cannot do for ourselves in the context of salvation.

Sources Used for *Hebrews*

Barnes, Albert. *Barnes' Notes* (vol XIII). Grand Rapids: Baker Book House [no date]; orig. published by Blackie & Son (London), 1885.

Coffman, James Burton. *Commentary on Hebrews.* Austin, TX: Firm Foundation, 1971.

Hailey, Homer. *God's Eternal Purpose and the Covenants.* Louisville, KY: Religious Supply, 1998.

Jamieson, Robert, Andrew Fausset and David Brown. *Commentary Critical and Explanatory on the Whole Bible (1871),* electronic edition. Database © 2012 by WORDsearch Corp.

Kistemaker, Simon J. *The New Testament Commentary: Exposition of Thessalonians, the Pastorals and Hebrews.* Grand Rapids: Baker Books, 1996.

Lenski, R. C. H. *Commentary on the New Testament: The Interpretation of the Epistle to the Hebrews and of the Epistle of James.* Grand Rapids: Hendrickson Publishers, 1998.

Lusk, David. *The God of the Covenant.* Mesa, AZ: [self-published], 2002.

Milligan, Robert. *The New Testament Commentary* (vol. IX). Delight, AR: Gospel Light [orig. published 1868].

Robertson, Archibald Thomas. *Word Pictures in the New Testament* (vol. V). Grand Rapids: Baker Book House, 1960.

Strong, James. *Talking Greek-Hebrew Dictionary,* electronic edition. Database © 2004 by WORDsearch Corp.

Wuest, Kenneth S. *Word Studies in the Greek New Testament,* vol. II. Grand Rapids: Eerdmans Publishing Company, 1947; reprinted 1992.

Endnotes

1   R. C. H. Lenski, *Commentary on the New Testament: The Interpretation of the Epistle to the Hebrews and of the Epistle of James* (Grand Rapids: Hendrickson Publishers, 1998), 9.

2   Lenski, *Interpretation*, 11.

3   It must be understood, however, that Nero's persecution was brief, particularly aimed at Christians in Rome (and vicinities), and thus relatively limited. Unlike persecutions that followed, Nero never instituted an imperial decree against all Christians everywhere or a systematic assault against the church.

4   James Burton Coffman, *Commentary on Hebrews* (Austin, TX: Firm Foundation, 1971), 18.

5   "At the beginning of the revelation, the presentation was elementary. Later it appealed to a more developed spiritual sense. Again, the revelation differed according to the faithfulness or unfaithfulness of Israel" (Kenneth Wuest, *Word Studies from the Greek New Testament* [Grand Rapids: Eerdmans Publishing, 1947], 32).

6   While *specifically* "last days" could refer to the end of the Jewish Age, being finalized by the destruction of Jerusalem in AD 70, the usage here is not specific. The writer is making a general contrast between how God revealed His will to believers *then* and *now*: "then" He spoke through the Law and the prophets (Deut. 18:18–19); "now" He speaks through His Son (Mat. 17:5). The fact that He *still* speaks through His Son today (through the gospel) indicates that the "last days" are not completed, but that we are still in them. There will not be yet another set of "days" in which we listen to someone other than God's Son; we are in the final revelatory age.

7   Specifically, through the Urim and Thummim ("lights and perfection"), the special breastplate worn by the high priest which was used to consult God for difficult decisions; see Exod. 28:30 and Num. 27:21.

8   The Father Himself is exempted in this transference of authority (1 Cor. 15:27–28). Even though Christ is given "all authority" (Mat. 28:18), He does not exercise authority over His Father, but the two work together as one (John 17:22–23).

9   The "Godhead" is not a biblical word but is a biblical doctrine. It refers to the holy, seamless, and incomprehensible union of the Father, His Son, and His Holy Spirit (see 2 Cor. 13:14, for example, where each member of the Godhead is mentioned separately). God "abides" in (or indwells) the believer through His Spirit and His Son (Rom. 8:9, 1 John 2:24). Whoever has fellowship with one member of the Godhead has fellowship with all of them.

10   We know Christ as "God's Son" because we would not understand His relationship to the Father in any other way. He is *like* a "son" in many respects. Yet aside from His earthly existence, He is *not* like an earthly son for the following reasons: He was not born, but has always existed (John 8:58); He has no mother; He possessed divine, creative power and authority even before He inherited His Father's kingdom; He never fails or disappoints His Father; and probably several other reasons. Furthermore, God the Son can die and be resurrected, but God the Father cannot die, which is why God the Father could not offer *Himself* as a sacrifice for men's souls.

11   This is from the Greek word *charakter* ("character") (A. T. Robertson, *Word Pictures in the New Testament*, vol. V [Grand Rapids: Baker Book House, 1960], 336; Wuest, *Word Studies*, 37–39). As one's character is the true image of who that person really is, so Christ's "character" is an exact image of the Father (John 14:7–9).

12   "Levitical" means, in essence, "a system of (the priests produced from the tribe of) Levi." Specifically, it refers to the high priests who ministered to the tabernacle/temple under the Law of Moses. According to the Law, only Levites could be priests, and only Levites descended from Aaron (a Levite) could be high priests.

13   Someone might question this, based on passages like Job 1:6 and 2:1, where the "sons of God" presented themselves before the Lord. However, the usage and context there is so general that literal *sonship* cannot be meant. God is "Father"—thus, *life-giver*—to all living beings; thus, every living, intelligent creature is His "son." Yet angels are no more *literal* (or begotten) "sons" of God than Timothy was a literal "son" of Paul (2 Tim. 1:2).

14   Heb. 1:5 quotes Psalm 2:7 and 2 Sam. 7:14; 1:6 quotes either Deut. 32:43 or Psalm 97:7; 1:7 quotes Psalm 104:4; 1:8–9 quotes Psalm

45:6–7; 1:10–12 quotes Psalm 102:25–27; and 1:13 quotes Psalm 110:1 (the most–quoted Psalm in the entire NT).

15 Lenski, *Interpretation*, 62.

16 First, consider the several references to the "angel of the LORD" in God's communication with men (as in Exod. 3:2). Second, the pillar of cloud (or fire) is referred to in this same way (Exod. 14:19, 32:34). Third, an "angel of the LORD" would lead Israel into battle against the Canaanites (Exod. 23:20, 33:2). The point is: God has used angels throughout the revelation of His law to His people, indicating that the Law, though revealed to earthly men, was of heavenly origin.

17 "The author is discussing this new order introduced by Christ which makes obsolete the old dispensation of rites and symbols. God did not put this new order in charge of angels" (Robertson, *Word Pictures*, 344).

18 The Greek word for "man" in this passage (2:6) is not *aner* (male), but *anthropos* (a generic term for a human being), in reference to mankind (Wuest, *Word Studies*, 56.)

19 The OT quotes in 2:12–13 are from Psalm 22:22 and Isa. 8:17–18.

20 Robert Jamieson, Andrew Fausset, and David Brown, *Commentary Critical and Explanatory on the Whole Bible (1871)*, electronic edition (database © 2012 by WORDsearch Corp.); on 2:14.

21 We should note that the writer does not regard Satan as a mythical boogeyman or an imaginary enemy, but as a real and identifiable personage. This is true of every reference to Satan in the NT.

22 At the same time, we are limited in our knowledge of this "death" since none of us has experienced it. "Until we understand perfectly what death is, we cannot of course fully understand its power" (Robert Milligan, *The New Testament Commentary*, vol. IX [Delight, AR: Gospel Light; orig. published 1868], 99).

23 Based on this passage (2:15–16) and others, Satan has been defeated, yet he still maintains a measure of power, influence, and control over people. This can be confusing to Christians who do not understand the context of his defeat. Satan has not been *removed from the picture* since we are still told to be on guard for his schemes (2 Cor. 2:11) and that he is still a threat to us (1 Peter 5:8). Some believe that Satan has been completely neutralized (often citing Rev. 20:1–3, a visionary scene) and that what we are experiencing today is merely "residual evil"

from what he sowed from many centuries before. Yet the NT gives a different picture—one that should not be ignored. Satan most certainly has been defeated by Christ through His death: He came to "destroy the works of the devil" (1 John 3:8) and He overcame Satan's *powers*. But this language refers to the "works" and powers that Satan has over believers who have chosen to draw near to God (James 4:7–8). By severing our allegiance to Satan in our baptism into Christ, we rob him of his full power over us and allow Christ to lead us instead.

24 The reason for this is because all salvation from sin is obtained through faith in God—a faith that has not yet seen the One who saves but believes in Him (Heb. 11:1–2, 6). Angels that sin, however, have already dwelt in the presence of God and therefore cannot exercise faith: no one needs faith (or hope) for what he has already seen (Rom. 8:24–25). Instead of being offered salvation, angels that sin are simply condemned and await a future judgment (2 Peter 2:4, Jude 1:6).

25 This alludes to the Levitical high priest's role in the Day of Atonement (Lev. 16), in which atonement was made for the entire nation of Israel. The student of *Hebrews* would do well to read and become well–acquainted with that event. The writer not only draws on it heavily throughout his epistle, but the Day of Atonement ritual also serves as a primitive yet effective illustration of Christ's mediatory role for His church.

26 "Propitiation" (2:17; see Rom. 3:25, 1 John 2:2, and 4:10) alludes to the OT use of the word "covering," the same as is used to describe the lid [lit., mercy seat] of the ark of the covenant. Synonyms include "expiation," "satisfaction," and "atonement."

27 "High priest" is used 17 times in *Hebrews* in reference to Christ, but nowhere else in the NT is He referred to in this way.

28 When someone asks, "Did Christ's blood fulfill the requirement of the Law of Moses, or did it inaugurate the law of Christ (i.e., the gospel)?" the answer must be *yes*. His blood accomplished both things at once: it brought closure to the one while establishing the other. It is incorrect to say that we are under God's covenant with Israel (or that we are under the Law of Moses), because we are under a new covenant that has superseded that one. However, it *is* accurate to say that Christ's blood provides a crucial link to the two covenants.

29 Lenski, *Interpretation*, 105.

30 Robertson, *Word Pictures*, 353.

31 For a detailed exposition on grace, I recommend my book *The Gospel of Saving Grace* (Waynesville, OH: Spiritbuilding Publishers, 2020); go to www.spiritbuilding.com/chad.

32 This is a specific reference to a specific act: the Creation. In other words, because He rested from *that* work (since it has been completed) does not mean He rests from *all* work (that remains ongoing), or that He does not have *any* work (an idea of which is the underpinning of Deism).

33 We cannot help but think of Christ, who fully carried out all the work which God had given Him and thus had every right to rest from His earthly ministry (John 17:4–5, 19:30). Not only does this point undermine modern Premillennialism (which claims that Christ must return to earth for another 1,000 years of work) but it inarguably proves that Christ's work was indeed "once for all," as the writer later declares (Heb. 10:10, etc.).

34 This means that one must *act in obedience to the command of God.* This plea is not limited to those who have yet to become Christians; in the present case (as in the case of 2 Cor. 6:1–2), it applies to those who have already believed, but who are in danger of being unbelieving. God gives His grace freely to those who so respond, but His grace is "in vain" to those who turn away from Him toward anything else.

35 Milligan, *Commentary*, 139.

36 I recommend my book, *The Holy Spirit of God: A Biblical Perspective* (Waynesville, OH: Spiritbuilding Publishers, 2010) for a much fuller explanation of this passage; go to www.spiritbuilding.com/chad.

37 "Teachers" here does not necessarily mean literal Bible class teachers but refers to those who actively promote the gospel's teaching in whatever way is needed and appropriate; see 2 Tim. 2:2.

38 Obviously, subjects like "washings" (likely a reference to baptisms or purification rites beyond what was required to become a Christian), "laying on of [the apostles'] hands" (likely, the transmission of miraculous gifts in general), the future resurrection of the saints, and "eternal judgment" were challenging believers in the first century as they continue to challenge people today. These subjects deserve intelligent and biblical responses, to be sure. On the other hand, the Scriptures offer

limited information on them and will never satisfy everyone's questions. The point here seems to be this: learn what you can from the Scriptures, revisiting these teachings as needed, but do not be immobilized by teachings that, in the end, do not change the message of salvation or our moral responsibility to God.

39   The allusion here is to the cities of refuge, where one guilty of involuntary manslaughter was able to seek protection from the "avenger of blood" (Num. 35). In that scenario, he had to remain in a city of refuge until the death of the high priest. Likewise, the Christian seeks refuge in Christ from the Avenger of our souls—for our having been responsible for the death of His Son—but since our High Priest never dies, we are forever safe in Him.

40   Lit., a tithe; "a tenth of the top of the heap" of the spoils—i.e., the best part (Kistemaker, *Exposition*, 187).

41   It is this statement ("he lives on") and the one in 7:16 ("indestructible life") that have led some to assume that Melchizedek must be of divine origin, and that he is in perpetual existence, like Christ (John 8:58). Yet there is nothing in *Hebrews* or the rest of Scripture to validate such a bold claim or its serious implications.

42   Consider John the Baptist's reference to Jesus in John 1:30 as a related case in point.

43   Perhaps the principle of the curse to rebuild what God has destroyed would apply to "rebuilding" the Law of Moses as it did to the rebuilding of Jericho (compare Josh. 6:26 and 1 Kings 16:34). Just as no man is to separate what God has joined together (Mat. 19:6, in principle), so no man is to resurrect what God has destroyed.

44   God "will not change His mind" on this; or, as the KJV says, "will not repent." On this, Milligan aptly writes: "When God is said to repent, the meaning is that he simply wills a change; and when it is said that he will not repent, it means that he will never will a change. And consequently, there is nothing beyond the priesthood of Christ to which it will ever give place, as a means of accomplishing God's benevolent purposes in the redemption of mankind" (*Commentary*, 210).

45   God's ultimate proof that His special relationship with Israel is over was demonstrated in His judgment against Jerusalem in AD 70 (see Luke 19:41–44, 21:20–24). That event completely destroyed the

temple, which nullified sacrificial intercession, rendering the priesthood unworkable, and thus made obedience to the Law of Moses impossible.

46   James Strong, *Talking Greek–Hebrew Dictionary,* electronic edition (database © 2004 by WORDsearch Corp.), G4241.

47   The fact that we are in the "last days" (Heb. 1:2) confirms this: there will not be another (new) dispensation in which we will need a different priest(hood), and thus a different law. What we have in Christ is final, all–sufficient, and will continue until the literal end of time.

48   This was done during the Day of Atonement; see Lev. 16.

49   It is true that Jesus was circumcised on the eighth day, thus inducting Him into God's covenant with Israel (Luke 2:21). But this covenant was a *national* covenant, not a *personal* one; all its promises were meant for the Israelite community (see Deut. 28:1–14, for example), not solely for the individual believer. In other words, Jesus did not subject Himself to God's covenant with Israel because He was a sinful person but because He was indeed *an Israelite*, "born of [an Israelite] woman, born under the Law" (Gal. 4:4).

50   Slight differences to the text in Jeremiah are because the writer of *Hebrews* quotes from the Septuagint rather than quoting from the Hebrew Bible. This is the case in virtually every OT citation in this epistle.

51   In fact, this phrase resonates throughout the entire Bible: Exod. 6:7, Lev. 26:12, Jer. 31:33, 2 Cor. 6:16, Rev. 21:3, etc. What God has always wanted—and continues to seek—is a loving relationship with those who believe in Him. This objective is paramount to all other objectives; it is the underlying motive for all God has done in bringing salvation to mankind.

52   Just because men and women are equal in covenant standing does not mean that all the gender–specific roles—in life, marriage, and the church—are nullified. Men still have the responsibility to be husbands, fathers, and leaders and workers in the church; women still have their roles as wives, mothers, and workers in the church. The equality "in Christ" (Gal. 3:28) is how *Christ* sees us in a spiritual context, without respect to our earthly roles.

53   Due to a misunderstanding of this verse, many Christians think that God literally *forgets* about our sins. Given God's divine nature—

He knows *everything* and forgets *nothing*—this cannot be true. If there are facts, historical information, or *any* information outside of His knowledge, then He cannot be "God," as there would be something more powerful than Him that is preventing Him from knowing this information. When God says "I will remember" (see Gen. 9:16, Exod. 6:5, and Lev. 26:45 for example) or "I will *not* remember," He is not saying, "I will suddenly recall what I had forgotten" or "I will choose to never think of this again." Instead, He is saying, "I will take *action* on what has been said (or promised or done in the past)" or "I will *not* take action" on something that He knows *has* happened. An excellent example of this is in Jesus' parable of the unmerciful slave (Mat. 18:23–35). That slave was forgiven by the king—it could be said that the king "remembered this man's debt no more." But after hearing of the slave's unmerciful treatment of a fellow slave, the king *reinstated* the debt and held him accountable to pay it back in full. Jesus ended that parable by saying "My heavenly Father will also do the same to you" if anyone does not forgive his fellow believer. Just because crimes are forgiven does not mean they are literally forgotten from memory. Likewise, the debt of our sin is not literally forgotten, but it is forgiven *if* we maintain the conditions by which this forgiveness was offered in the first place.

54   At first glance, it appears that the writer says (in 9:4) the altar of incense was located *within* the Holy of Holies, when in fact it was not (Exod. 30:6, 40:26). Certainly, he was not confused, having already demonstrated his expertise in these matters. The seeming contradiction can be easily remedied by understanding that the altar of incense was so closely connected with the Holy of Holies, it was identified with it (1 Kings 6:22). And, to access the Holy of Holies, the high priest had to first burn incense on the golden altar (Lev. 16:12–13): the one was necessary to partake of the other.

55   Solomon's temple also had two huge statues of cherubim in the Holy of Holies (1 Kings 6:23–28).

56   The first veil was the one at the entrance to the first (or outer) sanctuary; the "second veil" (9:3) is the one between the first sanctuary and the second sanctuary, which is the Holy of Holies.

57   Some believe the rod of Aaron was set *beside* the ark, given Num. 17:10, but we have no reason to dispute what is written here in 9:4.

58   "The writer states that the Holy Spirit is both the divine Author of the Levitical system of worship and its Interpreter" (Wuest, *Word Studies*, 154).

59   "It is not of course meant that he literally *bore* his own blood into heaven—as the high priest did the blood of the bullock and the goat into the sanctuary…but that that blood, having been shed for sin, is now the ground of his pleading and intercession for the pardon of sin—as the *sprinkled* blood of the Jewish sacrifice was the ground of the pleading of the Jewish high priest for the pardon of himself and the people" (Albert Barnes, *Barnes' Notes* (vol XIII) [Grand Rapids: Baker Book House; no date; orig. published by Blackie & Son in London, 1885], 192).

60   At this point (9:13–14), the writer alludes to a different sacrifice than the Day of Atonement (the offering of "bulls and goats"). The "ashes of a heifer" refers to the elaborate cleansing ritual (the so–called "red heifer ordinance"—see Num. 19) for those who had become defiled through contact with death (i.e., a dead body or a grave). In that ritual, a flawless red heifer was ceremonially slain and then burned to ashes; these ashes were mixed with water and then sprinkled upon the one defiled by death to cleanse him. (The full cleansing ritual took seven days to complete.) Being defiled by death and being corrupted by sin are parallel situations: both make fellowship with God impossible.

61   This cleansing is not accomplished apart from the believer's own participation. In 1 Peter 3:21, for example, we learn that baptism (i.e., immersion in water) is the *believer's* role in cleansing his conscience. His is an act of faith; Christ's is an act of grace. Christ does not baptize people, and people cannot cleanse their own conscience apart from the sprinkling of His blood. Thus, Christ *and* the believer must act accordingly.

62   It is unfortunate that we use "testament" rather than "covenant" to define the gospel message ("New Testament"). For one, "testament" is not as accurate as "covenant"; for another, if we spoke of the "New Covenant" (as Jesus did—Luke 22:20), then so much of the foreignness of our *relationship* with God would be removed, and we would emphasize this relationship so much more (versus focusing on the trappings and liturgy *of* that relationship—i.e., church services, church protocol, etc.). For a better understanding of "covenant," I recommend

(but do not endorse every conclusion of) *God's Eternal Purpose and the Covenants* by Homer Hailey (Louisville: Religious Supply, 1998); and *The God of the Covenant* by David Lusk (Mesa, AZ: [self-published], 2002.

63 Blood indicates the vicarious sacrifice of the one being offered. One life is given for another; the sinner lives only because of the life offered in his place. In the old economy (the Levitical system), an animal's life sufficed for this transaction; in the grand scheme of things, however, only the blood of a perfect Son of Man—One who was also the Son of God—could satisfy God's ultimate requirement for justice.

64 Under the Law, a very poor man could bring a bloodless sin offering (Lev. 5:11–12) but the priest still had to make atonement for him (5:13), which necessarily implied a blood offering from another source. Ultimately, the Day of Atonement sacrifice would cover all such omissions. Thus, "the *memorial* was made with flour, but the *atonement* with blood" (Milligan, *Commentary*, 262; emphasis is his).

65 This is also the ultimate implications in passages like 1 Sam. 15:22 and Mic. 6:7–8.

66 From the Greek word *paroxusmos* (Wuest, *Word Studies*, 182).

67 "The Greek word (the noun) is used nowhere else in the New Testament, except in 2 Thessalonians 2:1, where it is rendered *gathering together*. The verb is used in Matthew 23:3 Matthew 24:31, Mark 1:33, 13:27, Luke 12:1, 13:34, in all which places it is rendered *gathered together*. It properly means *an act of assembling*, or *a gathering together*, and is nowhere used in the New Testament in the sense of an assembly, or the church. The command, then, here is, *to meet together* for the worship of God, and it is enjoined on Christians as an important duty to do it" (Barnes, *Notes*, 234; all emphases are his).

68 "Two or three witnesses"—not necessarily *eyewitnesses* but those who are capable and competent to serve as a kind of grand jury—are sufficient to evaluate and render a verdict concerning a particular case; see Deut. 17:6–7 and 19:15.

69 See Zech. 12:10, the only other time "Spirit of grace" is used in Scripture. In that context, God promised His "Spirit of grace" to His people so that they would recognize the One who was "pierced" for them.

70   The quotes in 10:30 are from Deut. 32:35–36 and are part of the Song of Moses which was regularly sung as part of Jewish synagogue worship.

71   "Prisoners" here (10:33–34, as in Heb. 13:3 and Mat. 25:36) does not refer to people imprisoned for ungodly crimes, but believers imprisoned for their *faith in Christ*.

72   Milligan, *Commentary*, 291.

73   "Confidence" here is from the Greek word *parresia*, which is often used with reference to the boldness of one's speech and outspoken public admission (Strong, *Dictionary* [electronic], G3954; Vincent, *Word Studies* [electronic], on 10:35). Thus, the Hebrews' confidence was not merely a loss of heart within; it was also a lack of proclamation without—i.e., a refusal to publicly defend Christ and His gospel as *God's truth*. Christ will not reward anyone who refuses to defend Him before men—for any reason (Mat. 10:32–33).

74   Judaism had been around for some 1,500 years, while Christianity had existed for less than 40 years. One might argue that Judaism had *proved* to be far more enduring than Christianity; therefore, a return to Judaism was understandable. However, this fails to consider all the arguments made thus far, as well as Jesus' predictions that the Jewish system was about to be permanently terminated.

75   For a comparable passage, see 2 Peter 3:3–9, where "mockers" based their entire conclusions upon what they were able to see, not on what had been promised (by a God who had already fulfilled every promised He had ever made to date).

76   The popular argument against Creation usually boils down to this: there is no science to support it. Ironically, there is no science to support the Big Bang Theory, the Theory of Evolution, or the Theory of Everything, but this does not stop intelligent people from believing in this. Faith in God is predicated on physical, moral, and eyewitness evidences (including the written record of Scripture), not scientists. Even though Creation preceded science, the laws of physics and energy are natural expectations of an all–powerful and all–intelligent God who alone could design them.

77   The implication in the Gen. 4 account is that blood sacrifice was not only required as part of God's covenantal relationship with His

people but had also been instructed in some manner. Neither Cain nor Abel were acting on their own in providing these offerings; they were responding to a command that has not been recorded for us. This command had to have had specific requirements for God to have approved of one but rejected the other.

78 While it appears from some translations that Sarah is suddenly mentioned on par with Abraham (11:11), the original Greek text's grammatical construction does not support this. It is Abraham's faith which is and remains the specific focus here. This is not to say that Sarah had no faith, but she did not have the power to conceive apart from Abraham's own faithfulness, and Abraham is the one to whom God made the promise. The margin reference for 11:11 in NASB reads, "Lit., power for the laying down of seed," which demonstrates the power of the male and not the female—thus, the faith of Abraham, not Sarah (Kistemaker, *Exposition*, 323).

79 In a sense, they *did* comply with the decree—they put their son in the Nile River—but not with the intention that Pharaoh had implied. Pharaoh's decree called for the Hebrew boys' destruction by drowning; Moses' parents sought the preservation of their son's life.

80 Not the Zechariah who authored the book by this name but a different prophet (2 Chron. 24:21–22).

81 Kistemaker, *Exposition*, 355, fn. 69.

82 Lit., "died by sword–slaughter," implying a mass–execution rather than an individual one (Wuest, *Word Studies*, 210); yet either of these meanings would support the writer's intention.

83 This can be translated literally "testifiers"; it is from the Greek *martures*, from which we get "martyr" (Strong, *Dictionary* [electronic], G3144).

84 Consider also that being "hanged on a tree" represented a curse (Deut. 21:22–23 and Gal. 3:13–14); thus, Christ bore the reproach of one who was (said to be) cursed.

85 "Striving" is from the Greek word *antagonizomai*, "to struggle against," and alludes to Grecian contests of boxing or wrestling in which the opponents would be covered with blood from the ferocity of their struggle (Strong, *Dictionary* [electronic], G464; Barnes, *Notes*, 294).

86 Lenski, *Interpretation*, 435.

87   Another possibility also exists: sons who are not disciplined have an irresponsible and unloving *father*. But in the case of God, this is impossible, since "God is love" (1 John 4:8) and is thus fully responsible toward those entrusted to Him *and* always acts in their best interest. Given this, the alternative is not even pursued here.

88   The words here are similar to Prov. 4:26–27 and Isa. 35:3–4.

89   James Macknight writes: "A root of bitterness is a person, utterly corrupted, and who by his errors and vices corrupts others" (quoted in Coffman, *Commentary*, 324). Just as the root ultimately reveals its true nature in the form of a plant, the corrupted soul will be revealed in that person's earthly actions (Mat. 7:15–20, in principle).

90   One has to wonder why the writer brings up *sexual sins* (implied in "immoral") to a group of Hebrew Christians who very unlikely had anything to do with these. But immorality is the natural result of a "godless person," as the apostle Paul revealed (Rom. 1:21–27). Perhaps the writer is saying: "If you forfeit your reward in Christ by turning away from Him—something only a godless person would do—then do not be surprised at what kind of illicit behaviors this will ultimately produce, even in yourselves." In any case, the warning has full force to us today: any godless attitude, behavior, or belief system is inherently *immoral* in nature. Esau serves as a timeless parable of what this looks like and what one loses in the process.

91   The "no place to repent" phrase brings us back to the thoughts discussed in 10:26–27. Esau lost all opportunity to regain his first–born inheritance since Isaac would not change his mind (see Barnes, *Notes*, 304, and Coffman, *Commentary*, 327–328). This is not a comment on the state of Esau's eternal soul; nonetheless, it appears that a person can reach a point in his lifetime when he forfeits all opportunity for repentance to God and *will* lose his soul. Just because we cannot know *when* (or *if*) someone crosses this line does not mean the line does not exist or cannot be crossed.

92   The implication here is also that of the generation of Israelites who died in the wilderness, who failed to listen to the voice of God as revealed through His servant Moses (Num. 14:22–23; see 1 Cor. 10:5).

93   This passage seems to serve as a dual prophecy: it speaks of an ultimate "shaking" (or sifting), but this does not prevent other lesser

(but significant) upheavals in the meantime. One such upheaval was clearly the destruction of Jerusalem (AD 70), which marked the termination of the Law of Moses, its sacrificial system, the Levitical priesthood, and the privileged status of Israel toward all other nations. All these things God once created; all these things God has since removed. But the kingdom of God—the reign and realm of Christ's authority in which the church has been established—*will not* be shaken, since it is eternal and indestructible (Dan. 7:13–14).

94 Lenski, *Interpretation*, 468.

95 This fact recalls what was said in 10:34; see Mat. 25:39, Acts 28:30, and 2 Tim. 1:16–17.

96 JFB, *Commentary* (electronic), on 13:5.

97 The writer quotes from Deut. 31:6, 8 or Josh 1:5, then from Psalm 118:6.

98 While Jesus (in John 6) did *not* speak of or describe the Lord's Supper directly, one cannot help but make a connection between the two ideas. Jesus spoke to the Jews of internalizing His character and His doctrine; yet later He instructed His disciples to "remember" Him in a simple memorial that symbolizes the eating of His body and drinking of His blood. An unbeliever—a non–follower of Christ—has no right to participate in this memorial.

99 The gospel makes a clear distinction between the people of the "true circumcision" (i.e., Christians) and the people of physical circumcision (i.e., unbelieving Jews) who are under a curse; see Rom. 2:28–29, Gal. 6:12–16, Phil. 3:2–3, and Rev. 2:9.

100 We see the same effect in Jesus' healing of, say, a leper (Mat. 8:2–3). According to the Law, since a leper is unclean (Lev. 13:45–46), whoever touches a leper also becomes unclean and must be ritually purified. Yet Jesus did not become unclean because He possessed the power to *heal* rather than merely *touch*. In a real sense, He overcame the leper's uncleanness by removing it entirely (see also Luke 7:11–15). Similarly, Jesus overcomes the sinner's uncleanness by removing his sin entirely, having absorbed *in Himself* the justice required for it.

101 Compare parallel passages in Acts 20:28, 1 Thess. 5:12, 1 Tim. 3:4–5, and 5:17.

102 "The obligations of the Church and of her officers, are mutually binding. If it is the duty of the Elders to teach, it is also manifestly the duty of the other members of the Church to receive their lawful instructions; and if it is the duty of the former to rule, it is equally the duty of the latter to submit to all their acts of discipline which are not in violation of the law of Christ" (Milligan, *Commentary*, 380–381).

103 Yet Paul does warn that such men ought not to be questioned without sufficient evidence or witnesses. Bringing charges of sin against an elder is not impossible to do, but it is a most serious matter, given his leadership over the group and the effect such accusations will have *upon* that group (1 Tim. 5:19–21). I have much more to say on this subject in my *1 & 2 Timothy* and *Titus* commentaries; go to www.spiritbuilding. com/chad.

www.ingramcontent.com/pod-product-compliance
Lightning Source LLC
LaVergne TN
LVHW010320070426
835513LV00025B/2434